Natural Prayers

Natural Prayers

Chet Raymo

Hungry Mind Press
Saint Paul, Minnesota

Published by Hungry Mind Press
1648 Grand Avenue
Saint Paul, MN 55105

10 9 8 7 6 5 4 3 2 1
First Hungry Mind Press printing 1999

Printed in the United States of America

ISBN: 1-886913-29-3
Library of Congress Catalog Number: 99-72103

Cover art: Betsy Bowen
Cover design: Randall Heath
Book design: Wendy Holdman
Typesetting: Stanton Publication Services, Inc.

To Nils Bruzelius
and
Kathy Everly

Contents

Acknowledgments

I thank Pearl Kilbride, Page Cowles, Gail See, and all the good folks at Hungry Mind Press for their support of my work. Brigitte Frase, Amy Bell, Mary Byers, Betsy Bowen, and Dallas Crow applied their special talents to this book. My agent, John Taylor Williams, found the manuscript a sensitive home.

As in everything I write, the influence is felt here of Nils Bruzelius and Kathy Everly of the *Boston Globe*, who by skillful editing of my columns for that newspaper over many years taught me much about writing. The support of the Lannan Foundation and Stonehill College is deeply appreciated.

Introduction

The earliest prayer I can remember is, "Now I lay me down to sleep, I pray the Lord my soul to keep." Head on pillow, tiny palms pressed together, parent sitting close at hand, I sleepily mumbled the words, "If I should die before I wake, I pray the Lord my soul to take." The prayer was formulaic. It might as well have been a nursery rhyme or a string of made-up sounds like *abracadabra*. It was, in fact, an incantation, a magical plea to the powers of the universe to guide me through the little sleep of night into the light of another day.

I was raised in a culture of petition, inculcated from an early age with a repertoire of formulaic prayers addressed to God, his angels, or his saints. All of the prayers assumed a response: *Here I am, Lord, deserving of your attention, favor, healing, forgiveness*. Never did it pass my mind that my prayers were not heard. My education was hemmed about with a huge body of stories affirming God's intervention in human affairs. Had not every religious person experienced firsthand the power of prayer—a return to health, a financial difficulty resolved, a lost object found? Were not the shrines full of abandoned crutches? Did not every chapel gleam with votive candles lit in thanks? The evidence of efficacy was overwhelming.

Or rather, the evidence of the efficacy of prayer appeared overwhelming to a mind predisposed to belief. Later, I trained as a scientist and also studied the history and philosophy of science. I learned something about controlled experiments, the statistical analysis of data, and the appropriate exercise of educated skepticism. Most important, I learned how belief can influence judgment—even the judgment of scientists—and how scientists strive to *minimize* the role of belief in the evaluation of evidence. No knowledge system can be entirely free of personal and cultural predispositions, which is why scientists place so much emphasis upon peer review, mathematics, diagrams, photographs, specialized language, and the strict exclusion of personal religious, political, and philosophical affiliations from scientific communication.

In the light of my new scientific skepticism, the evidence for the success of petitionary prayer became a thing of smoke and mirrors, a compilation of mere anecdote. Of course, believers in the power of petitionary prayer will not be dissuaded from their belief by the dearth of respectable scientific support; after all, God in his omniscience may simply refuse to cooperate with any rational analysis of his power. However, many persons, such as myself, who are skeptical of miracles and respectful of experiment, are left with rather a hole in our lives. We were taught that God hears and answers prayers; a careful examination of the evidence reveals no compelling measure of response.

For many of us, that hole in our lives has been filled by a new story of the creation that does not require a God who intervenes in day-to-day affairs. It is an evolutionary story that reaches inward to embrace the ceaseless dance of DNA and outward to the spiraling galaxies, a story that places human life and consciousness squarely in a cosmic flow of complexifying energy. This new story is thoroughly grounded in the science of our time, but open to revision as we learn more. The Roman Catholic priest and cultural historian Thomas Berry urges us to assimilate the new story into our religious and prayerful lives: "The universe, the solar system, and the planet earth in themselves and in their evolutionary emergence constitute for the human community the primary revelation of that ultimate mystery whence all things emerge into being." For Berry, the significance of the scientific creation story is this: the universe is a unity, an interacting, evolving, and genetically related community of beings bound together in an inseparable relationship in space and time. Our responsibilities to each other, to the planet, and to all of creation are implicit in this unity, and each of us is profoundly implicated in the functioning and fate of every other being on the planet.

In the traditional cosmology of my youth, an Olympian God, who is separate from his creation, hears and responds to our individual prayers; in the new scientific cosmology, God reveals himself in and through his creation, as law and chaos, light and darkness, creator and destroyer. In the words of the Jesuit theologian David Toolan, God is "the Unnameable One/Ancient of Days of the mystics, of whom we can only speak negatively (not this, not that), a 'wholly other,' hidden God of Glory." Or again, in the words of the Greek novelist Nikos Kazantzakis: "We have seen the highest circle of spiraling powers. We have named this circle God. We might have given it any other name we wished: Abyss, Mystery, Absolute Darkness, Absolute Light, Matter, Spirit, Ultimate Hope, Ultimate Despair, Silence. But we have named it God because only this name, for primordial reasons, can stir our hearts profoundly. And this deeply felt emotion is indispensable if we are to touch, body with body, the dread essence beyond logic." The God of the new story does not take note of our childish cries for attention. Rather, we are swept along on the grand wings of an abiding plan and presence.

How do we pray in such a universe, to such a God? The Trappist contemplative Thomas Merton wrote: "The option of absolute despair is turned into perfect hope by the pure and humble supplication of monastic prayer." He defines monastic prayer as "a prayer of silence, simplicity, contemplative and meditative unity, a deep personal integration in an attentive, watchful listening of 'the heart.'" Learning to pray, then, as I understand it, is learning to listen with the mind and heart—making oneself *attentive* to each exquisite detail of the world. It is a fearsome, exhilarating task, best suited to solitude and silence. Such prayers are answered not with miracles, tagged with our names or those of our loved ones, but with beauty and terror. For the prayerful listener, the world becomes the sublime scripture, full of stories of structure and chaos, law and chance, complexification and decay, including the story of the human person in whom the universe becomes conscious of itself.

All of my life has been a relearning to pray—a letting go of incantational magic, petition, and the vain repetition "Me, Lord, me," instead watching attentively for the light that burns at the center of every star, every cell, every living creature, every human heart. What follows is a breviary of "natural prayers," meditations inspired by mindfulness to the natural world, unfolding during the course of a year, following the seasons of sun and moon. They celebrate three different landscapes where I spend part of each year—the island of Exuma in the Bahamas, the environs of a New England village, and the wild, rocky Dingle Peninsula in the west of Ireland. The seasons are represented by the solstices and equinoxes, and the less familiar "cross days," halfway between the solstices and equinoxes, which have made their way into our secular calendar as Groundhog Day, May Day, Lammas (a harvest festival celebrated in Europe), and Halloween. Each meditation springs from something seen; my purpose is to discern the extraordinary in the commonplace, to find that "dread essence beyond logic." This book is full of science because knowledge is a prerequisite for love. "Less and less do I see any difference between research and adoration," wrote the great Jesuit theologian Pierre Teilhard de Chardin near the end of his life. For Teilhard, as for many poets and mystics, prayer is a meditation on the world, informed by knowledge, open to mystery. It is in this sense that I call these meditations "natural prayers."

Exuma

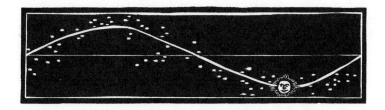

Winter Solstice

 New Moon

"To pay attention, this is our endless and proper work," writes the poet Mary Oliver. I'm trying, I'm trying. I have spent the last hour of late afternoon on the porch floor watching an army of ants move a dead moth. The ants are as tiny as grains of salt, their legs and antennae barely visible to the unaided eye. The moth is the size of a double postage stamp. It is like watching a crowd of humans attempt to shift a 747 jumbo jet by the power of muscles alone. What the ants lack that humans might exploit is the ability to act in concert. No foreman directs their efforts. They fidget. They flurry. They scurry under and around the moth even as they heave and push. They come and go, apparently at random, laboring momentarily, then dashing off. They are the antithesis of concert. Yet somehow the moth moves toward the edge of the porch with an almost imperceptible inevitability.

It is the solstice. I am on the island of Exuma in the

central Bahamas, seeking respite from the New England winter. A new moon's tide licks the rocks at the top of the beach. The sun slides to its western rest. I'm down on my belly with the ants. Where are they going? To what nest? Some common purpose keeps the dead moth moving in a foreordained direction, although to my gaze the ants seem to be pushing in every direction at once. Clearly they are communicating. But how? A language of strokes and prods? A tickling of antennae? A vocabulary of chemical traces, emitted and received, each molecule locking into an appropriate sense receptacle, like lock and key, triggering an impulse to the ant's brain? Ensconced in a subterranean larder, the moth will be a copious food supply. I imagine the moth labeled with "Nutritional Information," like a loaf of bread or box of cornflakes: carbohydrates, protein, vitamins, fat. The ants fidget. They flurry. Any passerby would stop to watch a crowd of humans attempting to move a 747; the ants and the moth are an equal spectacle, differing only by a matter of scale.

The moth moves across the porch, millimeter by millimeter, a brief stage of a longer journey of energy from the core of the sun to the table of the ants. Protons fuse at the center of the sun, releasing energy. The energy diffuses upward, taking several million years to reach the sun's surface, where it is released as heat and light. The light streaks across ninety-three million miles of space, reaching the Earth eight minutes later, where it falls upon the green leaves of plants. The plants store the energy as carbohydrates. A moth stops at a flower of a plant and sips the sugary nectar. It uses the nectar's stored energy for flight, reproduction, and building a body rich with organic compounds. The moth beats its brains out against my porch light and falls dead to the floor, where it is discovered by a scout of a colony of ants. The call is raised: "Food!" Now the rest of the colony arrives, at first in ones and twos, then en masse. A storm of purpose ignites their tiny brains. Humping their backs and fiddling their legs, they have a go at the moth. The moth drifts across the porch floor, taking the packaged energy longer to cross a few feet of painted boards than it took to travel from sun to Earth.

It is a feature of the way the world is made that two protons together have less mass than two protons separately. This is a startling but indisputable fact. Weigh two protons separately, then weigh them together: the numbers don't match. The numbers differ by about 1 percent. This curious difference is not to be explained by some law of nature; it *is* a law of nature, as basic to the way the world works as any fact in our possession. The mass discrepancy is equivalent to an amount of energy given by Albert Einstein's formula $E = mc^2$, where c is the velocity of light. The velocity of light is a big number; squared, an even bigger number. A tiny mass difference is equivalent to a huge amount of energy. Make protons stick together and you have access to this energy. There's a catch, however. Protons have positive electrical charge, and like charges repel. To make two protons stick, you must overcome the electrical repulsion that drives them apart. You must get the protons close enough together so that a short-range but powerful nuclear force comes into play. The nuclear force is the glue that holds protons together.

Nowhere on Earth is there sufficient force to overcome the electrical repulsion of protons and make them stick together, except in a few hugely expensive particle accelerators and fusion reactors—and in the fury of atomic bomb explosions. However, protons are easily squeezed together at the centers of stars: all that huge weight pushing down. Protons fuse at the center of the sun and 1 percent of their mass is turned into energy. There is a famous line by the poet Dylan Thomas: "The force that through the green fuse drives the flower." Thomas was more right than he realized. That word: *fuse.* Fusion is the force that drives the sun, and sunlight drives the flower. The energy of proton fusion at the sun's core flows upward, through half a million miles of the sun's bulk. It percolates through the sun's seething interior, absorbed and reradiated again and again. As the energy approaches the solar surface, it is carried along by the churning mass of the sun itself, in huge convective loops of hot gas. At last, at the furiously roiling surface, the energy is hurled into space as heat and light. Every second at the sun's core 700 million tons of protons—the nuclei of hydrogen—are fused together. Every second five million tons of proton mass disappear from the universe, replaced by an amount of energy equal to the missing mass times the speed of light squared. Every second the sun throws five million tons of its own substance into space as radiant energy. The sun never misses so tiny a fraction of its bulk. The sun has been burning steadily for more than four billion years, and in all of that time it has used up less than a thousandth of its mass.

Every second, five million tons worth of energy is

thrown into space by the sun. Eight minutes later, one two-billionths of that energy is intercepted by Earth. That's five pounds worth of the sun's vanished mass that falls every second upon the Earth. About a billionth of an ounce's worth of that energy falls upon my three-quarter-acre plot of land on the island of Exuma, where it is absorbed by palms, palmettos, coco plums, sea grapes, sea oats, bur grass, beach grass, and beach morning glories. The plants photosynthesize, building carbohydrates. Moths sup and die. Ants devour moths. Frogs eat ants. Humans eat coco plums. Sand flies eat humans. The energy is shared around. Our little community of flora and fauna sucks up every last drop of that billionth of an ounce of the sun's missing mass, that "force that through the green fuse drives the flower." Dylan Thomas and Albert Einstein were contemporaries. They died within a few years of each other in the mid-1950s. Poet and scientist, they perceived the essential unity of matter and energy. They recognized in nature a force that drives all things, creative and destructive, holy and terrible. Its source is the sun.

Here, on this three-quarter-acre patch of land, I am part of a full web. Bat moth. Free-toed frog. Ani. Ant. Brown racer snake. Snail. Mouse. Woodstar hummingbird. A swarm of mostly unidentified flying insects at night about every outside light. Adorable gecko and abominable sand fly. We are all of us dependent upon one another, and utterly dependent upon a curious property of protons that is built into the foundation of the world. Mostly we go through life oblivious to the source of animation. To trace the web—to follow the energy up and out of the sun, across ninety-three million miles of space, down through a cascading chain of plants and animals—requires paying close attention. "Ancient religion and modern science agree," writes John Updike. "We are here to give praise. Or, to slightly tip the expression, to pay attention." Scientists know a lot about paying attention; attention is our business, our raison d'être, down on our bellies, noses to the moth. And what is more natural than to speak of the beauty we see? John Ruskin wrote in *Modern Painters:* "The greatest thing the human soul ever does in this world is to see something, and to tell what it saw." Exact description is the highest praise.

 First Quarter Moon

A photograph in the book review section of the journal *Nature* shows three moths drinking from a trickle of liquid that flows from a huge glistening eye. The caption says, "The Asian moth *Hypochrosis baenzigeri* makes an elephant cry and then drinks its tears." Let me repeat that: "The Asian moth *Hypochrosis baenzigeri* makes an elephant cry and then drinks its tears." I have no idea how moths provoke an elephant's tears, why the tears are more to be desired by the moths than nectar or plain water, or what benefit, if any, accrues to the elephant from this curious arrangement. But the photograph and the caption stick in my mind, lingering somewhere between ecology and poetry.

First, there is the startling contrast in scale between the

elephant and the moths: the elephant's eye is twice the size
of an individual moth—a great dark pool from which flows
a river of tears. Second, there's the poetic tension between
tears and nourishment. But more than contrasting scale,
more than poetry, it is the *interdependence* of moth and elephant that I can't shake from my mind, the sad and beautiful evocation of symbiotic life on Darwin's tangled bank.
The word *symbiosis* (two or more different organisms living
together in mutually advantageous association) was coined
more than a century ago, in an 1877 scientific paper on
lichen anatomy. Lichens consist of a cohabiting alga and
fungus. The alga photosynthesizes carbohydrates, upon
which the fungus feeds. The fungus supplies the alga with
useful minerals. Neither organism is capable of existing
independently unless supplied with the proper nutrients;
together, they are hardy enough to survive harsh environments where neither creature could exist alone—the snowy
tops of mountains, the margins of glaciers, desert rocks.

Symbiosis is a driving force of evolution. Biologist
Lynn Margulis was the first to suggest that the many-
compartmented eukaryotic cell—of which all multicelled
animals and plants are composed—was a product of symbiosis. The oxygen-respiring units of eukaryotic cells,
called mitochondria, resulted when respiring bacteria were
incorporated symbiotically into larger microorganisms that
lacked the ability to respire; the mitochondria gained a reli-
able food supply, the host cell gained the advantages of res-
piration. Similarly, the hairlike appendages of eukaryotic
cells called flagella, which give cells motility, likely origi-
nated as thin undulating bacteria that latched onto larger

cells for feeding, found the arrangement satisfactory and never let go; the host cells gained propellers. Ditto for the photosynthesizing units called chloroplasts; what began as symbiosis became unity. The alliance of three or four simpler microorganisms for mutual benefit created a supercell that swept all before it. Every cell in my body is a eukaryote, as are the cells of the ant, elephant, moth, and other multicelled organisms. In "The Lives of a Cell," Lewis Thomas wrote: "If it is in the nature of living things to pool resources, to fuse when possible, we would have a new way of accounting for the progressive enrichment and complexity of form of living things." There's that word again: *fuse.* It is not yet clear to biologists how much of this tendency to pool resources is in the nature of living things and how much is merely useful evolutionary accident. I am inclined to believe that the tendency to fuse, to combine resources, *to complexify,* was there at the beginning, in the aftermath of the Big Bang—an inevitable consequence of the way the world is put together.

Nowhere is the *inevitability* of symbiosis more vigorously contested than in the scientific debate about Gaia. The Gaia hypothesis (named for the Earth goddess of the Greeks) is closely associated with Lynn Margulis and the British scientist James Lovelock. It proposes symbiosis on the scale of the planet, embracing all creatures great and small, from elephant to moth, from great blue whale to bacterium, together with rocks, air, and oceans, regulating the planetary environment so as to make it optimal for life. Gaia is a superorganism, say Margulis and Lovelock, as large and as old as the Earth itself, of which we are all parts, as our cells are parts of our own bodies. Many scientists consider the Gaia hypothesis far-fetched, based more on wishful thinking than observation, and without a causal mechanism to make it work. Others see Gaia as a powerful insight into the way of the world, a new metaphor to replace the "world as machine" metaphor that has guided science for the past four hundred years. All thinking is metaphorical. In science as in poetry, we understand by making analogies. We are always on the lookout for analogies that unify our experience of the world. Is the Earth a clockwork ticking according to the laws of mechanics, as Newton and his successors supposed, or is it a living organism, as the Gaians propose? Is the world best understood by breaking it into its component parts, as one might take apart a clock to see what makes it tick, or as an *indivisible unity*, a living organism? Of course, the terms of the questions are not mutually exclusive; any strategy that engages our attention with the world is likely to be useful. Nevertheless, the organic metaphor has begun to change the way we perceive and understand the world, focusing our attention on *fusion, symbiosis, community.*

For the moment, the world-as-machine metaphor remains dominant in science, and perhaps properly so, for it has proved to be a vibrant way of attending to nature's patterns. But what is appealing about the world-as-organism metaphor is the way it draws us into poetic alliance with the objects of our attention. As when I lie on my belly and watch a determined troop of ants shift a moth across the floor of the porch. As when I read, "The Asian moth *Hypochrosis baenzigeri* makes an elephant cry and then drinks its tears."

◯ Full Moon—Old Moon

It is perhaps a conceit on my part to imagine that I am part of a web that includes the ant, moth, gecko, sea grape, palm. I have a neighbor on the island who, to build his house, cleared his property with a bulldozer. Scraped it clean. Down to bare coral rock and sand. Not a blade of grass left standing. We humans have that much power. Nothing can bear our assault if we set our minds to destruction. But it is not just physical force that binds us to our fellow creatures. Our spirits, too, are linked. I do not mean to sound mystical. I am not talking about spirits as the disembodied souls of traditional religion, or as the vague cosmic resonances of New Age philosophy. I am talking about heart and mind as they are embedded in *matter*. When we cut our hearts and minds free from the web of life—from the green fuse—we sever our roots, and something fierce and flowing ceases to animate us. Our souls may be inextricably entangled with our bodies, but they are not bounded by the envelopes of our bodies. Our souls have roots in the ages, in the fusion of protons at the heart of the sun, in the burgeoning multiplicity of life. Our spirits throw out tendrils. We send runners. The growth of our spirit is—can be—lush, tropical. Our souls are bounded only by the limits of our knowledge. As I write, a giant bat moth is splayed against the stucco of the terrace wall outside my window, dark on light, six inches wide from wing tip to wing tip, the surface of its wings a mottled wavy brown. The Cubans call them *brujas*, "witches," and believe them to be the embodied spirits of the dead. In the Bahamas, too, they are greeted with trepidation. This particular bat moth has remained stationary for an hour, illuminated by the light of a rising full moon, its wings spread like two black hands in supplication. I think of another line of the poet Mary Oliver: "If you notice anything, / it leads you to notice / more / and more."

Harvard biologist E. O. Wilson has coined a name for the human love of other species: biophilia. Biophilia is our best hope for survival and happiness on this planet, he says. But how am I to love the other creatures with which I share this three-quarter-acre plot of rock and sand: the scorpions, for example, which inevitably attract a quick whack with the heel of a shoe, or the sand flies, which we swat and spray without remorse. The ethics of biophilia are complex and subjective. The trick, I suppose, is to distinguish love from squeamishness. We eat meat, but we are happy to let someone else do the slaughtering. We understand that deer herds must be culled for their own good, but we are unable to look down the barrel of a gun into the eyes of a white-tailed doe. Scientists kill many animals in the course of medical and biological research, and most of us are content that they do so. Death is the terrible and necessary corollary of life. Ants require the death of the moth. The free-toed frog requires the death of ants. Death is nature's way of portioning out the energy, wringing the rag of energy dry, exploiting every ounce of vanished mass at the core of the sun. Like symbiosis, killing is a creative engine of evolution. Certainly, for many of us, not having to look our victims in the eyes makes killing more palatable.

Our hummingbirds are cherished. Our geckos are welcome, as long as they stay out of our bed. The bat moth ditto. Mice—well, when I came to the island I started out with traps, until I looked into their sad Disneyesque eyes, accusing me from beneath the sprung wire. And the ants—ah, yes, the ants. What do we do about the ants, tiny sand-colored ants, as small as grains of salt? This morning I found them in the sugar bowl, a seething swarm. A marching line of ants stretched down the side of the bowl, across the cupboard shelf, down the wall, along the countertop, back up the wall to a crack in the plaster that leads to who-knows-where. I disposed of the contents of the sugar bowl. Then I took a wet sponge and obliterated the line of marching ants, all the way back to the crack, a clean murderous swipe that must have smushed a thousand lives. It is hard to find much to love about the churning, despicable mass of insects that invaded my sugar bowl. The Latin word for ant is *formica*. Formic acid, widely used in industrial processes, occurs naturally in the bodies of ants. ("Would you be calm and placid," rhymes Ogden Nash, "if you were full of formic acid?") From the Latin root we also have the scientific name of the ant family, Formicidae, and a bunch of other ant words, such as *formicary* (a nest of ants), *formicate* (to swarm with ants), and *formication* (an abnormal sensation of ants crawling over the skin). The very sight of that formicating formicary in my sugar bowl was enough to make my skin crawl. Biophilia, my eye. *Swish* with the sponge. A few hours later the marching army is reestablished, this time fixed on some grains of sugar I had inadvertently lift on the counter. Another *swish*, another thousand lives.

But now curiosity was getting the best of me. I carefully killed every ant in sight. Then I placed a pinch of sugar at a new location and went for a walk. When I came back, the marching army was established on a new course, anchored on the pinch of sugar. From the crack in the wall, which may be far from the nest, scouts fan out looking for food. One of them stumbles upon a source of nourishment—a pinch of sugar. It finds its way home, presumably following the chemical equivalent of Hansel's line of bread crumbs, where it communicates its discovery, then leads its myriad companions back across a vast desert of walls and countertops crisscrossed with chemical tracks. This sophisticated feat of navigation and communication is accomplished with a brain the size of a pinpoint. "The universe is not rough-hewn, but perfect in its details," wrote Henry David Thoreau in "The Natural History of Massachusetts"; he was talking about ants. Ants employ the most complex system of chemical communication of any animal, according to E. O. Wilson and Bert Holldobler, Harvard entomologists and the world's foremost experts on ants. Ants are jam-packed chemical factories, their glands endlessly active, puffing or squirting secretions for every purpose. *"Follow me, I've found sugar."* *"This way, this way!"* When tastes and scents fail, they have other modes of communication—tappings, strokings, graspings, nudgings, and antennations—an unabridged dictionary of ant gab. Sometimes ant communication runs dangerously amok. Wilson and Holldobler describe a group of army ants that was cut off from the main foraging party: the soldiers of the group were so strongly attracted to each other that they formed a "mill," going blindly round and round in each other's tracks for a day and a half until all fell dead.

Not rough-hewn, but perfect in its details. That tiny brain. Those multiple secretory glands. That little thread-like nexus that attaches the back half of the ant's body to the front half (wasps get credit for the "wasp waist," but ants are no less pinched in the middle). Ignoring this perfection of detail, I sweep up the ants with the sponge and lay out more bait to see what will happen. Murder has become research. "Nature will bear the closest inspection," continued Thoreau; "she invites us to lay our eye level with the smallest leaf, and take an insect's view of the plain." I soap down the walls and counter tops to eliminate chemical tracks. I put out pinches of sugar and watch and wait. I look for scouts. I want to see the marching army emerge from the crack. I want to observe their habits of communication. Nature has no interstices, said Thoreau; every part is full of life. Even in its tiniest manifestations, life and intelligence are miraculous and beautiful. I wait, I watch. I pay attention. My respect for the ants grows. My sponge makes its killing journeys with increasing reluctance.

 Last Quarter Moon

Walking home in the moonless Bahamian night from drinks at our local bar, we suddenly felt ourselves whirled into infinity. And it wasn't the drink. The Earth curved away under our feet, placing Orion higher in the sky than we were used to seeing him in New England—twenty degrees higher. Canopus lifted its light above the horizon at Orion's feet. Canopus is the second-brightest star in the sky, after Sirius, but too far south to be visible from Boston. Suddenly we felt the *roundness* of the planet, as if we could stand on tiptoe and see the Southern Cross—the stars of the Australian flag—waiting to rise, just there, over the southeastern horizon. The winter Milky Way was a river of light arching from north to south above our heads, passing near Orion's back—the gathered brilliance of the myriad stars that make up our galaxy, individually invisible to the unaided eye. Our sun is two-thirds of the way out from the center of the pinwheel galaxy. In winter, our view is toward the edge of the pinwheel, so the river of light is not so luminous as on a summer evening when we face the star-packed center. The winter Milky Way is lost in the lights of Boston, but here, in the pitch dark of a sparsely populated island, it was prominent. Most extraordinary of all was a mysterious lobe of light that reached halfway up to the zenith from the place on the western horizon where the sun had set. At first we thought we might be seeing the lights of the airport, until we realized that our tiny airport could never make such a far-reaching glow. We were seeing the zodiacal light, brighter than I ever remember seeing it before.

The zodiacal light is caused by sunlight reflecting from meteoric dust that orbits the sun in the plane of the solar system, remnants of the vast nebula of dust and gas out of which the solar system was born more than four billion years ago. Like the planets, this diffuse stream of particles reflects light, although faintly and rarely seen. Moonless nights of winter are the best time to see the zodiacal light, and nowhere better than here, on the Tropic of Cancer, where the plane of the solar system is tipped so as to pass directly through our zenith, lifting the band of faint light up and away from the horizon. And so we were treated to the spectacle of two intersecting rivers of lights, the light of two great whirling disks, the solar system and the galaxy. The solar system is tipped on its side within the greater disk of the galaxy, so the two rivers of light intersect more or less at right angles. The axis of the Earth is tipped within the solar system, and our bodies were tipped with respect to the axis of the Earth. We struggled to orient ourselves to these many cockeyed angles. In the twenty minutes we stood gaping at the light-streaked sky, our spinning planet carried us 350 miles to the east. The flight of the Earth around the sun whirled us 22,000 miles through the space of the solar system. The turning galaxy bore us 200,000 miles through the cosmic abyss. We felt like the prophet Ezekiel, who saw in the heavens intersecting wheels turning upon wheels, sparkling like chrysolite. It was enough to cause vertigo.

Do they matter, these moments of singular insight into deep space and deep time, these gifts of grace that come unbidden—the curving Earth, the arching luminous planes of solar system and galaxy? John Calvin, stern father of the Reformation, wrote in 1559, not long after Copernicus sent the Earth careening around the sun, "The powers of the soul are far from being confined to functions that serve the body. Of what concern is it to the body that you measure the heavens, gather the numbers of the stars, determine the magnitude of each, know the space that lies between them, with what swiftness or slowness they complete their courses, how many degrees this way or that they decline?" There are activities of the soul that have no practical use, suggests Calvin. Measuring the heavens will not put a Porsche in the driveway, or an Olympic-size pool in the backyard. On the first day of my astronomy classes I tell my students, "This course will not help you make a buck." Few students run for the door. What draws them to astronomy is not greed but a longing of the soul to know its place in the universe.

In the twenty minutes that we stood under the stars, we made a flight of more than half a million miles across the cosmos, whirled on circles within circles. We were star travelers, trekkers of infinity, Ezekiel meets Mr. Spock. Nothing practical, nothing that will help pay the bills. Just a long interval of rapturous contemplation of the objects of the soul's longing.

 New Moon

The Big Bang! First there is nothing. Then an infinitely dense, infinitely hot kernel of energy that expands explosively. Space-time inflates like a balloon that was infinitely small at the beginning. Where does it happen? Everywhere. When does it happen? As time begins. The universe expands and cools. Energy becomes matter, at first quarks, electrons, and neutrinos; later the quarks will form protons

and neutrons. One-hundred-thousandth of a second after
the beginning, the universe is a seething stew of particles
and radiation. Fifteen seconds after the beginning, the temperature has cooled to a billion degrees and the creation of
matter settles down. After 700,000 years, protons and electrons bind together to make atoms of hydrogen and helium.
Later still come stars and galaxies. The term *Big Bang* was
coined in 1950 by the astronomer Fred Hoyle, a champion
of the so-called Steady State universe, in which things have
always been more or less as they are now, with no beginning or end. Back in 1950, the primeval fireball theory was
a bit of an upstart, and Hoyle dismissed it derisively as "the
Big Bang." His scornful label stuck, even as new observations eventually led to almost unanimous acceptance of an
explosive beginning for the universe. In 1993, astronomy
writer Timothy Ferris suggested in *Sky and Telescope* magazine the desirability of a new name for the universe's beginning. "Big Bang" is ugly, misleading, and trivializing, he
said; it is a name more suitable for a dormitory brawl than
for the gloriously luminous event that spawned the starry
skies. What is required, he said, is something more digni-
fied, more accurate, less accidental in origin. Taking up his
challenge, the editors of *Sky and Telescope* invited readers to
rename the Big Bang, in a contest to be judged by Timothy
Ferris, Carl Sagan, and Hugh Downs. The magazine received thirteen thousand submissions. In the end, they decided that nothing had quite the currency or panache of
"Big Bang."

I never made a submission to the contest, but I gave
the matter some thought. I quickly dismissed names like

Alpha 1, Cosmodawn, Uniseed, GENesis, Apsutime (from
Apsu, the Babylonian begetter of gods), or Protophos
(from the Greek for *first light*); these all sounded a bit like
supermarket products. What is required, I decided, was
something with a bit of humor, something that doesn't take
itself too seriously. How about the Big Sneeze? A creation
myth from Egypt of the third millennium B.C. has God
bring the world into being with a sneeze. It's not a bad
image for the creation as it is currently described by astronomers. Fifteen billion years ago the universe began
with an outward explosion of pure energy. A blaze of
gamma rays, X rays, and light. Then particles, atoms, stars,
and galaxies. A spray of material creation. *Ahh, ahhh, ahhhh-
CHOO!* The Big Sneeze. Better than the Big Bang. More
poetic, more firmly grounded in the ancient human quest
for origins. And more evocative of an explosion from nothing. "Big Bang" suggests a firecracker exploding in pre-
existing space and time. But space-time came into existence
along with the universe, the way a sneeze sometimes comes
out of nowhere. Or how about the Big Ha? God's laugh. A
great roaring belly laugh that brings all things into being.
An ancient Jewish creation text has God create the world
with seven laughs. The first laugh is light. A blazingly luminous hoot of laughter. A side-splitting guffaw of gamma
rays, X rays, and a rainbow of colors. The Big Ha puts a little fun back into creation.

Or better yet, the Big Speak. Among ancient myths,
the Word is one of the most universal images of creation.
In the beginning was the Word, and the Word was made
flesh. Christians have tended to appropriate the Word to

themselves, but it can also be found in creation stories of the Mayans of central America, the Maoris of New Zealand, and the Wapangwa of Tanzania. God speaks, and the word becomes the world. "The Word was not something that could be seen," says the Wapangwa myth. "It was a force that enabled one thing to create another." Exceedingly apt. The Big Speak. But *Speak* sounds terribly pompous. Like a sermon. Like a snooty pronouncement. How about something more whimsical? Raven, the trickster god of the Eskimos, creates the world with a bit of mischief. Let Raven be the one who speaks. A wonderful, explosive, glottal call. The Bird-Word. Ancient. Universal. Tongue-in-cheek. An infinitely fulsome *cr-r-r-cruck* of creation. The Big Squawk.

In late 1995, the Hubble Space Telescope pointed its camera at a speck of dark sky between the stars and left the shutter open for a total exposure of ten days. It recorded galaxies fainter than any seen before, two thousand galaxies in an area of sky no larger than the intersection of crossed pins held at arm's length. We see the most distant of these galaxies at the era when the first galaxies were forming from the hydrogen and helium created in the Big Bang—or Big Squawk!—when the universe was less than 5 percent of its present age, less than a billion years old. The Cosmic Background Explorer (COBE) microwave satellite telescope has seen even deeper into the abyss of time. It has recorded the light of the Big Bang itself, a background radiation filling the entire sky, coming to us from a time about three hundred thousand years after the beginning. We will never see deeper into time than the COBE image of the sky. Before the universe was three hundred thousand years old, high-energy protons of light collided vigorously with protons and electrons in a hot soup called a plasma. The plasma is opaque, just as the glowing gasses inside a fluorescent lightbulb are opaque. It is impossible to see through the plasma to an earlier era.

So is God's spoken "Let there be light," the singular moment of creation, forever beyond the reach of scientific investigation? Will the first great sneeze or "Ha!" only be heard in echo, like a myth that comes down to us from an unknowable time of prehistory? Not at all. The human imagination is more resourceful than that. We explore the first three hundred thousand years of creation by recreating the conditions of that time here on Earth. One way to recreate the early universe is to do it mathematically. This is the business of theoretical cosmologists who apply known laws of matter and energy to the extraordinarily hot conditions that existed in the early universe. We can also use high-energy accelerating machines to speed up particles of matter to the staggering energies of the glowing primordial plasma. This can be extraordinarily expensive; the machines cost billions of dollars to build and run. But without doing the experiments, our mathematical theories remain just stabs in the dark. A team of physicists at CERN, the European particle accelerator lab, believe they may have reproduced the state of matter that existed when the universe was only ten microseconds old. By smashing lead nuclei into subatomic targets, they may have created a quark-gluon plasma, the precursor of protons and neutrons in the unfolding creation. Quarks are the constituent components of protons and neutrons. Gluons are the particles that hold them together. Ten microseconds! Ten microseconds after the first instant of creation! And already the universe had a knowable history. Already the universe had dramatically cooled from the infinite temperature of time zero. Already it had ballooned in size from an infinitely small point. Already the forces of nature had split from their initial godlike unity.

Does this stuff make your head spin? It made our heads spin as we stood in the ebony darkness of an Exumian night, spilling toward infinity. We let our imaginations fall into the third dimension, into deep time—planets, stars, galaxies, the radiant microwave energy recorded by the COBE satellite—through the vertiginous past toward the singular instant of creation. *Let there be light. Let there be . . . Let there . . . Let . . . L . . .*

 First Quarter Moon

"If the stars should appear one night in a thousand years, how men would believe and adore," wrote Ralph Waldo Emerson, "and preserve for many generations the remembrance of the city of God which had been shown. But every night come out these envoys of beauty, and light the universe with their admonishing smile." Emerson was a New Englander and should have known better than to say that the stars come out every night. The average cloud cover in New England is about 60 percent; that is, nearly two nights out of three are likely to be cloudy. Even in the least cloudy month of the year, October, a New Englander has only about a fifty-fifty chance of seeing stars. Things are considerably worse in Ireland, where I spend my summers; I am grateful for one starry night in ten. Which is no small part of the reason why I have begun to spend part of each year on a tropical island with few lights. Here, under cloudless skies undiminished by tungsten glow, the stars glitter in crystalline darkness. Objects I have elsewhere observed with telescope—the Beehive Cluster in Cancer, the Double Cluster in Perseus, the Andromeda Nebula—are here revealed to the unaided eye. Even the elusive zodiacal light, arcing upward from the western horizon in the evening and from the eastern horizon in the predawn darkness, teases the mind into contemplation of ultimate mysteries—and especially, the singular mystery of creation. The darkness of our night sky, it turns out, is itself a revelation of our origins.

The story of our origins—the story of the unfolding of the universe from an infinitely small, infinitely dense, and infinitely hot seed of energy—could never have been derived from observations with the unaided eye, or even with a small telescope or binoculars. Large national telescopes, expensive spectrographs, satellites, massive computers, and high-energy particle accelerators have been important in piecing together the story of the Big Bang. But there is a sense in which the beginning of the universe is available to all. Every stargazer who has looked into the night has made one of the most important observations in all of astronomy. The night sky is dark! The moon, planets, and stars shine in a black sky. We take the darkness of the night for granted. It is the stars, galaxies, and radiant nebulae that we suppose reveal the universe; night is a mere backdrop for luminous objects, like the black velvet cloth upon which a jeweler displays his glittering wares. But there is more to the darkness than backdrop. The absence of light in the space between the stars is as full of meaning as the stars themselves.

In 1610, the astronomer Johannes Kepler received a copy of Galileo's little book *The Starry Messenger*, reporting the Italian scientist's telescopic observations of the sky, including the discovery of myriad tiny stars twinkling beyond the limits of the unaided eye. Galileo claimed that the universe might be infinite and contain an infinite number of stars. Kepler protested. If this were so, he wrote Galileo, the entire celestial sphere would blaze with light as brilliantly as the sun. In an infinite universe filled randomly with stars, no matter which way we look our line of sight must eventually terminate on a star, just as a person in a wide forest must in any direction eventually see the trunk of a tree. Since the night sky is manifestly *not* as bright as day, the universe cannot be infinite, concluded Kepler. His argument was reasserted in mathematical fashion by Heinrich Olbers in 1826 and came to be known as Olbers's paradox: if the universe is infinite and randomly sprinkled with stars, there should be no night.

There have been many attempts to resolve the paradox. Some scientists suggested that if space were not empty, then interstellar gas and dust would absorb the light of distant stars; but it can be shown that the absorbing matter, if it exists, would eventually become hot enough to reradiate the same energy and therefore maintain the brightness of the sky. The discovery that stars are clumped in galaxies also fails to resolve the paradox; Kepler's argument can be applied to galaxies as well as stars. More recently, the expansion of the universe and the finite age of the universe have been considered as ways to account for the darkness of the night. According to present theories, the universe began about fifteen billion years ago in a Big Bang explosion from an infinitely small, infinitely hot seed of energy. The explosion didn't happen somewhere, it happened everywhere. Space and time came into existence with the universe itself. Since the first moment of creation, the texture of space has been inflating, like the expanding surface of a balloon or a rising loaf in the pan. Galaxies formed early in the history of the explosion, and they are carried apart with the expansion of space, like dots on the inflating balloon or raisins in the rising loaf. The expansion of the universe weakens the light of distant galaxies. As the galaxies race away from us, their light is stretched and cooled. Computer studies show, however, that the expansion of the universe dims the light of distant galaxies only by about a factor of two, not enough to account for the darkness of the night.

Then what about the finite age of the galaxies? The universe had a beginning, about fifteen billion years ago. Space may be infinite, but time had a start. Because light travels at a finite velocity, there is a limit to the part of the universe that we can see. We can't see galaxies that are more than fifteen billion light-years away because there hasn't been enough time for their light to reach us. Even if the universe is infinitely big, the part of it that we can observe is finite, and therefore the number of stars and galaxies we can observe are finite—and this is the true resolution of Olbers's paradox. *The night sky is dark because the universe is young!*

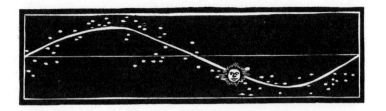

Groundhog Day

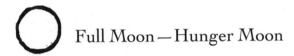 Full Moon — Hunger Moon

The Milky Way hangs like a sash at Orion's back, a river of stars in the ebony night. The moon rises, two days past full, and the river fades in its pearly light. Sash. River. Night. Moon. "Perhaps we are here only for saying: House, Bridge, Fountain, Gate . . ." says the poet Rainer Maria Rilke. These are good words, life words, lapped with memories of happiness and pain. They touch something deep within us. The poet continues: "But to *say* them . . . oh, to say them more intensely than the Things themselves ever dreamed of being." It is the poet's task to infuse such simple words with grander meaning. Scientists, too, must communicate their discoveries with the language of ordinary life: heart, milky, fountain, gush.

And so the headlines we read in the news:

"Fountain of Antimatter Discovered in Milky Way"
(*Washington Post*)

29

"Milky Way's Heart Gushes Antimatter" (*Science News*)

"Antimatter Found Gushing from Milky Way"
(CNN Interactive)

"Annihilation Fountain Found in Milky Way" (Reuters)

We respond. The words touch us. *Antimatter* suggests the future, the mysterious, potentiality. *Milky Way* is home, the enclosing sky, nourishment. *Fountain* is refreshment, rebirth, the Garden of Eden. Without quite knowing why, we are excited by the story. We want to know more. Here is the universe on the grandest scale, spilling its secrets into our own lives.

In 1927, the English physicist Paul Dirac, pondering the equations that govern subatomic particles, predicted that every particle should have a kind of mirror image, or "antiparticle." The electron, with its negative charge, should be complemented by an antielectron, or positron, alike in every respect except for having a positive charge. The positively charged proton should be complemented with a negatively charged antiproton. And so on. According to Dirac, the laws of physics implied that antimatter should—or could—exist. And if it does exist, then positrons and antiprotons can form antimatter atoms. Antimatter atoms can make antipeople, antiplanets, antistars, antiworlds. There is just one problem: If matter and antimatter come into contact, they will annihilate each other in a burst of pure energy, called gamma rays.

Five years after Dirac's startling prediction, positrons were produced in the laboratory. Today, at high-energy particle accelerator labs, the production of antimatter is commonplace. These antimatter particles are born into a world of matter. Almost instantly, they meet their matter complements and vanish in a puff of gamma energy. It takes lots of energy to make antiparticles. They vanish of their own accord.

As far as astronomers know, the observable universe is made almost entirely of matter, not antimatter, and this presents a puzzle. Matter and antimatter should have been created in equal amounts in the furious first moments of the Big Bang. But if other parts of the universe are made of antimatter, we should see a flood of gamma radiation arising from mutual annihilation at the boundaries where domains of matter and antimatter meet. No such radiation is observed. So where is all the antimatter today?

Physicists have long pondered the problem and may have an answer. It seems that just before the universe was one millisecond old, matter and antimatter annihilated each other in a sweeping extinction. But a tiny asymmetry was built into the universe so that matter dominated over antimatter by one part out of 100 billion. Why the built-in asymmetry? In the first 100 billion-billion-billionth of a second of the universe's history, particles called X particles and their antiparticles were created in equal numbers. These began to decay into other particles—quarks and leptons (which include electrons and positrons). But the decay rates of Xs and anti-Xs are not equal, for reasons that are still not fully understood. Equal numbers of Xs and anti-Xs decayed into unequal numbers of quarks and antiquarks, electrons and positrons. Quarks and antiquarks linked up to form protons and antiprotons. As the universe expanded and cooled, a tiny preponderance of matter over antimatter was frozen in. When the epoch of annihilation ended, only matter remained.

All of this happened before the universe was less than a thousandth of a second old!

And now we discover a fountain of positrons gushing from the center of our own Milky Way Galaxy, thirty thousand light-years away. These are certainly not anti-matter particles left over from the Big Bang; they are being produced in prodigious numbers by some kind of super-energetic events taking place at the center of the galaxy, perhaps matter streaming into massive black holes. The antimatter positrons are squirted outward. They encounter electrons. Astronomers observe the same gamma radiation that physicists see on Earth when electrons and positrons meet in mutual annihilation, an energy 250,000 times greater than that of visible light. They observe this energy with a purpose-made gamma-ray telescope lofted into space from the surface of our planet.

We observe. We speak. We couch these colossal events in words: "Milky Way's Heart Gushes Antimatter." We give voice to a universe that is wild and strange beyond our imagining. A fountain of antimatter particles, three thousand light-years tall, spewing from the energetic center of the Milky Way Galaxy—mysterious, ephemeral, telling of the beautiful and terrible Creation itself, of forces and powers we may never fully understand. How can words communicate such knowledge?

Heart. Milky. Fountain. Gush. "Praise this world to the

angel," says Rilke. "Do not tell him of the untellable . . . Tell him *things*. He will stand astonished."

 Last Quarter Moon

On a clear island night, before the waning moon makes its late appearance in the post-midnight sky, the naked eye can just discern the Great Orion Nebula as a patch of fuzzy white light in the sword of Orion. It might easily be mistaken for a blurry star, but the light we see is the light of many stars, newly born, embedded in a cloud of glowing gas, the stuff of their birth. The Orion Nebula is 1,500 light-years from Earth. It is the closest and brightest of the nebulae that populate the arms of the Milky Way Galaxy. It is roughly spherical in shape and big enough to hold twenty thousand solar systems. There is enough hydrogen, helium, and other materials in the cloud to make ten thousand stars like our sun (our own sun and solar system were born in just such a nebula nearly five billion years ago). The light from the nebula comes mostly from the radiation of doubly ionized oxygen (green) and the alpha radiation of ionized hydrogen (red). The gas is made to glow by the energy of hot young stars.

In binoculars, the nebula is easily distinguished from a star, but the color is still milky white, limited by the color sensitivity of the human eye. In a moderate-size telescope, the nebula shines with an eerie green glow, and the eye sees hints of shape—a curled, luminous hand, with four jewel-like stars, the Trapezium, glittering in the palm. This is a showpiece object for professional and amateur astrono-mers, and never fails to elicit "ooohs" and "ahhhs" from first-time viewers. But the Great Orion Nebula really comes into its own on long-exposure photographs made with major observatory instruments. These reveal a stunning complex of stars in the trauma of birth, swaddled in vortices and streamers of luminous gas, knotted by gravity—a star cradle measured by light-years and charged with the energy of creation.

The colors of the nebula are as various as the photo-graphs. On Kodacolor 400 film, Orion's great cloud is plum and lilac, cerulean blue, and milky white. On Ektachrome 400 the nebula is apricot and red, tinted with deep ochers and browns. On Kodacolor 1000 film, it is mauve and amethyst, blushed with rose. All of these colors seem to reveal some aspect of the nebula's beauty, but most are arti-facts of the film; different emulsions are sensitive to dif-ferent parts of the spectrum. No one has taken more spec-tacular photographs of the Orion Nebula than David Malin, a British-born astrophotographer at the Anglo-Australian Observatory in New South Wales. Malin is quite simply the world's best professional photographer of the heavens. For his finest shot of the Orion Nebula, he used the 1.2-meter UK Schmidt telescope at Siding Spring, Australia, to make three single-color photographs on fourteen-inch-square glass plates, each with a different color filter, which were combined into one color image. Filters and emulsions were chosen to give a uniform response across the spectrum. The green glow that we see in a small telescope combines with the reds and blues of the typical Kodacolor prints to brown and yellow the light. The image reveals peach, rose, olive, and orange—and grays banked like ash against the black of space. These are presumably the colors we would see if we approached the nebula. Malin's portrait of the Great Orion Nebula evokes nothing so much as an etching by the mystic-artist William Blake—a portal to eternity flanked by angels with diaphanous wings. And indeed, this is a kind of portal. The hot young stars at the core of the nebula have burned away the side of their cocoon, allowing us to look deep into the furnace of creation. These stars are probably no more than 100,000 years old. We are witness to the interior of a furious workshop where gravity and fusion bring worlds into being. The Hubble Space Telescope's wide-field and planetary camera has not improved upon Malin's colors, but it has added spectacular detail to the nebula. We see stars wrapped in the swaddling gases of their birth, each knot of gas a new solar system afloat in a gaudy matrix of seething matter. Looking at the Malin and Hubble photographs together, I think of something Immanuel Kant said: "God has put a secret art into the forces of nature so as to enable it to fashion itself out of chaos into a perfect world system."

The human eye is a poor explorer of the night. The color receptors in the retina of the eye do not work well in faint light. That's why the universe we see at night is black and white, or nearly so. That's why the Orion Nebula appears to the eye as a white blur—for those of us with skies dark enough to see it. But we are no longer limited by our biological senses. New imaging technologies have thrown open a window on eternity. It comes as something of a revelation that the fuzzy white blur in Orion's sword is a seething cauldron of color, stirred by angels, spawning stars. So, too, does knowledge enhance the other faint lights of night: the Milky Way, the zodiacal light, the "Little Cloud" in Cancer, the Andromeda Galaxy, the Double Cluster in Perseus, and so on. Two things are required to truly see: love and knowledge. Without love, we don't look. Without knowledge, we don't know what it is we are seeing. With love the attentive observer will recognize that the middle star in Orion's sword is smudged, slightly different from its neighbors. With knowledge, the smudge becomes a window on the birth of stars.

 New Moon

Each of us has a premier sense, a window larger than the others. For me, that window is vision. It is not larger in physical size; the tactile organ, the skin, has a thousand times more surface area than the retinas of the eyes; rather, it is larger in the quality of the excitements evoked by faint stimuli. Acute sensation is not a mere counting up of receptor cells. It is an electrical and chemical pandemonium in the brain, stimulated by the senses, formed by knowledge, out of which the brain somehow constructs that most ineffable of things—the soul. Perception, writes Diane Ackerman, is a form of grace. In Catholic theology, one must be "disposed" to grace to receive it. We are disposed by love and knowledge. The prepared mind is open to creation: smell, taste, touch, hearing, and vision—five windows, thrown open, uncurtained, in all weathers. "Life showers over everything," says Ackerman, "radiant, gushing."

For me, no grace of perception has proved more elusive than the green flash.

The green flash is a momentary blaze of emerald light that sometimes appears at the top of the sun's disk as it rises or sets on a distant flat horizon. The flash is caused by re-fraction (bending) of sunlight as it passes through Earth's atmosphere. In effect, the atmosphere acts like a prism, spreading the sun's light into a series of overlapping col-ored disks, blue at the top, red at the bottom. Blue light is effectively removed from the spectrum by the great thick-ness of air we are looking through at sunrise and sunset, which is why the rising and setting sun appears red; the re-moval is accomplished by an effect called scattering, which is simply the bouncing aside of photons of light by mole-cules of air. When most of the red, orange, and yellow light in the sun's spectrum is blocked by the horizon, we see what's left—the flash of green. By all reports, the effect is beautiful and electrifying. I've been watching for the green flash for thirty years. I've watched over seas and deserts, from beaches and mountaintops. I've watched at sunrise and sunset. When we built our house in Exuma we in-cluded a porch, just off the bedroom, facing the place of the rising sun, where we could watch each morning for the green flash; we call it the Green Flash Porch. Sunrise and sunset in the tropics are times when the sky puts on its most spectacular displays of light. The atmosphere empties its bag of optical tricks: reflection, refraction, scattering, absorption. Clouds go technicolor. Things high up catch the rays of the horizon-hidden sun and so become visible. Satellites glimmer. Mercury and Venus make their appearances. A Midas treasure is there for the taking. I have waited for sunrise on the Green Flash Porch almost every morning I have been on Exuma—but with never yet a hint of green.

Years ago I wrote about my search for the green flash in a book called *Honey from Stone*. I have mentioned my search for the green flash several times in my *Boston Globe* column. Readers of the book and columns have sent photographs of the flash. Some correspondents described observations of the flash from such unexotic locations as Cape Cod and the coast of Maine. One person invited me to his home in the Caribbean where be claimed the flash was visible almost every evening (I was sorely tempted to accept). *Sky and Telescope* magazine occasionally publishes photographs of the green flash furnished by subscribers; one correspondent even reported seeing a mini green flash as Jupiter set behind a distant horizon. So why haven't I seen it? Will nature withhold her fine green grace until I am somehow properly disposed? Or am I just unlucky?

The sky is an ever-changing theater of optical wonders. Mostly, we go around with our eyes to the ground. After all, the ground is where we eat, sleep, socialize, and make a living. If we look up at all, it is only to see the sky as a backdrop for birds, airplanes, and pop flies to the infield. The sky constitutes half of our visual field, but mostly we keep our eyes lowered — and half of our universe goes unnoticed. The sky is the arena of angels, but to move at ease within it, we must deliberately cultivate our senses. I have trained my color vision on the almost imperceptible hues of stars. I have observed a dozen kinds of rainbows. Glories, sun dogs, the zodiacal light, the gegenschein, mirages, moon bows, noctilucent clouds, meteors, bolides, a stellar nova — I have seen them all. A few years ago I watched a thousand annular eclipses of the sun projected onto the pavement under a tree by a thousand pinhole gaps among the leaves; it was an astonishing spectacle, eclipses scattered like bright coins for the picking! Once, in Alaska, I witnessed a beautiful circumzenithal arc, a kind of wrong-way "rainbow" caused by fat ice crystals floating in the upper atmosphere; I counted it a once-in-a-lifetime thrill. Perhaps the grandest show I have seen in the sky was a display of the aurora borealis I witnessed from northern Indiana. The sky exploded with fluid color — curtains, streamers, and starbursts of light — green, red, violet, yellow, psychedelic, apocalyptic. Diane Ackerman says of vision: "To taste or touch your enemy or your food, you have to be unnervingly close to it. To smell or hear it, you can risk being farther off. But vision can rush through the fields and up the mountains, travel across time, country, and parsecs of outer space, and collect bushel baskets of information as it goes."

And so I wait, morning after morning, on my Green Flash Porch, watching for an emerald grace to rush across the eight light-minutes, the ninety-three million miles, between me and the sun. Waiting. Waiting. Out of scents, sound, flavors, touches, and sights we construct our souls.

It is a lifetime project, cultivating the five senses in order to distinguish our selves from the buzzing, blooming confusion of the world, until we are able to say with confidence, "This is me." From scraps of the perceived world, sifted and sorted by the brain, we define a boundary between "self" and "other." It is a leaky boundary, thank God, pricked with the five senses, permeable to physical sensation and to wonder, allowing the soul to flow in and out from world to self and back again. On Exumian mornings, clouds heap on every horizon, violet, then pink, then gold, as reflection, refraction, and scattering do their tricks of light. My vigil is not the self-absorption of the New Age, nor is it the cool detachment of science. On the Green Flash Porch, in the warm auroral breeze, my senses buzz with an electricity flowing from knower to known and from known to knower—this is "me," this is "other"—crafting a soul from transmuted light in the thrall of the senses.

New England

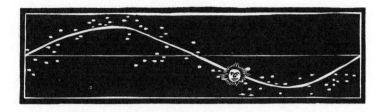

First Quarter Moon

Down along our New England brook, in trees by the water meadow, male red-winged blackbirds have taken up residence. We hear them before we see them, off there beyond the *tip-tip* of the nuthatch and the ice-pick *tunk* of the downy woodpecker, their voices a raucous intrusion upon the repose of the winter woods. Before the peepers, before the skunk cabbage, before the ice has melted in the shady margins of the brook, the red-winged blackbird announces spring.

It's not a pretty sound, the redwing's song. A bit of a frog in its throat. Like water forcing its way through a frozen pipe. A harbinger of spring should command a more sprightly song, more melodic, more forward-looking. But these things are subjective. Mabel Osgood Wright, who wrote about birds at the turn of the century, thought the redwing's song suggestive of "cool, moist ground and hidden springs." William Hamilton Gibson, another early writer, heard a felicitous "gurgle and wet ooze." These descriptions strike me as more hopeful than accurate. Listening to the redwing, Thoreau heard *conk-a-ree*. According to Emerson, "The redwing flutes his 'O ka lee.'" Turn-of-the-century ornithologist Frank Chapman has it *kong-quer-ree*, and Gibson heard *gl-oogl-eee*. Other writers transcribe the redwing's song as *gug-lug-geee, ookalee, onk-la-ree*, and *konk-la-reeee*. The only thing all these writers agree on is the final, drawn-out *eeeee*. Unmistakable, yes, but getting the red-winged blackbird's song reliably into a field guide has never been easy. F. Schuyler Mathews, in 1904, set out to do a better job. In his *Field Book of Wild Birds and Their Music*, he tried to transcribe birdsongs with musical notation. He gives the redwing's song as E, A, and trilled Cs in the key of A minor. However, Mathews adds: "To be sure the fellow is pardonably flat at times, and then again distressingly sharp; but on the whole the music is intelligible, welcome, and even inspiring, for it's a joyous announcement that spring is at hand."

Bird call descriptions of the early nature writers have an undeniable charm, but they proved to be of little use in advancing the science of ornithology. Music, like syllables on paper, can be frustratingly subjective, and science strives for objectivity. Electronic field recording of birdsongs has been possible since early in the century, but it was not until the 1950s that ornithologists acquired a way to reliably transcribe, exchange, and compare bird sounds. British ornithologist William H. Thorpe adapted for birdsong analysis a device invented at Bell Telephone Laboratories called a sound spectrograph, or sonograph. The sonograph breaks a birdsong down into its constituent frequencies and displays these as a graph of pitch versus time, called a sonogram. This breakthrough revolutionized the study of bird vocalization and turned a subjective semiscience into a respectable branch of biology. Anyone who doubts that much can be learned from sonograms should take a look at Thorpe's classic *Bird-Song* (1961), or Clive Catchpole and Peter Slater's *Bird Song* (1995). The subtlety and richness of bird vocalizations described in these books prove the adage that there are two musical races in the world—birds and humans.

Sonograms can be terrifically useful to the professional ornithologist, but they are not much help to the amateur birdwatcher. The redwing's song as displayed by Catchpole and Slater looks something like a woolly bear caterpillar marching across graph paper while shedding its coat. In the *Golden Field Guide to the Birds of North America*—the only popular guide that provides sonograms—the redwing's song is reduced to a smudge, between two and five kilocycles per second and about half a second long. Objective, yes. Romantic, no. Our typical response to the coldly impersonal sonograms is to turn away from science and stick with the amateur naturalist's *conk-a-ree*—to settle for the subjective, the anthropomorphic. At the same time, we can be grateful to the analytic scientists and their electronically recorded squiggles. Thorpe, who first applied the sonograph to birdsong, went on to write a classic book about learning and instinct in animals. His study of animal behavior eventually led him to consider the evolutionary basis of human moral behavior—from birdsong to Mozart, along an elastic string of time that binds us to all species. Without the cool objectivity of science, we listen to the redwing and hear only what we want to hear, an announcement of spring with a "gurgle and wet ooze," a mirror of our own hopes. With the knowledge science provides, we are also allowed to participate in an evolutionary drama larger and richer than ourselves, in which the human soul awakens in the course of deep time to a new season of consciousness and intelligence.

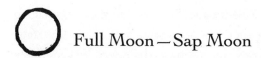 Full Moon — Sap Moon

Around our neck of the woods, the red-winged blackbirds return each year on February 27 — give or take a day or two. Not even a sudden ice storm or an unexpected warm spell delays their arrival. Their biological clocks are as punctiliously set as those of the swallows of Capistrano. I recognize the day of the redwing's arrival the moment I open my eyes from sleep, at precisely 6:00 A.M.; there is a certain timbre to the air, a certain ineffable anticipation of spring, a certain — ah, a certain twenty-seventh-ishness of February. The birds know, too. They know it's the twenty-seventh. A chemical ticking in their brains tells them so. They are perched in the trees by Queset Brook as I walk to work. I hear their throaty *chaaacck* even before I see them. I hear their *conk-a-ree*. The birds hunch forward, lift their wings, and flash their gaudy epaulets. They know the date. Their calendar is in their genes. And soon, as the season unfolds, other migrants also arrive—tree swallows, meadow-larks, bluebirds, sparrows, and warblers, each on its own schedule.

Birds bear within their bodies biological clocks that control the timing of migration, navigation, courtship, mating, and molting. These clocks are sensitive to changes in the environment; it is probably the increasing length of daylight, rather than temperature, that sets off the signal for the birds to leave their winter range in the southeastern United States and head north. Changes in light and darkness adjust the clocks, keeping them in phase with the day and season. If birds are kept experimentally in conditions of constant light and temperature, their internal clocks keep ticking with circadian (circa-dian, "roughly daily") and circannual ("roughly annual") rhythms. Anyone who has suffered from jet lag knows that biological clocks are not unique to birds. After a quick flight from America to Europe, for example, our internal clocks keep running on American time, and several days will pass before they are altered to agree with the new environment. Humans, mosquitoes, morning glories, even bread molds possess circadian clocks. Only the most primitive single-cell organisms appear to be without internal timekeepers. The sometimes faddish enthusiasm for biorhythms has a basis in biology. Timekeeping is the rhythm of the soul.

The mimosa plant was one of the first organisms to reveal its innate clock. In the 1700s, French scientists maintained mimosa plants under constant light conditions and discovered that the leaves continued to open and close at approximately daily intervals—although with a period of about twenty-two hours (the "roughly daily") instead of twenty-four hours. Without adjustment by exposure to natural patterns of light and darkness, the mimosa's clock runs somewhat fast. What are these internal clocks, where are they located, and what makes them tick? What is it that wakes me on the dot of 6:00 A.M., day in and day out? What causes the redwings to arrive reliably on February 27? If the pineal gland in the brain of a sparrow is removed, the bird loses its rhythmicity. If the pineal gland of a sparrow with twelve-hour "jet lag" (raised in conditions where the cycle of light and darkness is artificially reversed) is transplanted into another sparrow whose pineal gland has also been removed, the recipient takes on the rhythm of the donor. The pineal would seem to contain the pacemaker. But perhaps the pineal only bears necessary cues, like a radio time signal, for a clock that is located elsewhere, a clock that the recipient sparrow somehow quickly resets.

Hamsters are perfect for biorhythm research because their wheel-running activity, which normally takes place at night, is easy to monitor. Hamsters continue to take a daily run on a wheel even if kept in constant light. It is thought that the hamster's clock—and those of other mammals—lies in that part of the brain called the suprachiasmatic nuclei (SCN). In the absence of external stimuli, the rhythm of hamster circadian clocks is never less than twenty-three and one-half hours. Well, almost never. Martin Ralph of the University of Virginia found a mutant hamster with a twenty-two-hour circadian clock, from which he derived a line of short-rhythm offspring. He showed that he could shorten the rhythm of wheel running in normal hamsters by surgically excising their SCN and inserting SCN from fetal mutants—turning twenty-four-hour hamsters into twenty-two-hour hamsters. A more convincing demonstration of the biological nature of circadian clocks could hardly be imagined. I like to imagine my own circadian clocks ticking away in my SCN, like the vibrating quartz crystal of my watch, setting the beat of sleep, appetite, sex—the music of life.

There is still much that needs to be done in figuring out what it is that ticks and how it ticks, setting the metronome of the seasons. Locating the gene or genes that control circadian rhythm will help researchers find the answers. Meanwhile, the certainty that circadian clocks are internal and biochemical suggests certain whimsical modifications of natural rhythmicity. How about anti-jet lag pills that could be used to suppress circadian rhythms after a long flight, allowing for quicker resetting of the human biological clock? Or Saturday pills that slow the clock on weekends, allowing an extra hour or two of sleep? Or February 27 pills, bearing the ingredients of a finely tuned circannual rhythm (derived from the pineals of red-winged blackbirds) that would wake us an hour early on the day of the redwings's return, so that we could be there in the meadow when the birds stake out their territory, hear the first *conk-a-ree* of the reviving season, and marvel at the beat imparted to all creatures by a fine Swiss watchmaker called evolution.

Last Quarter Moon

The sap is rising. The last pockets of ice in the wooded swamp have thawed. Next week, on March 20, at 8:57 A.M. eastern standard time, the sun reaches that point on its annual journey where it crosses the equator into the northern celestial hemisphere. According to astrologers, this is the moment when the sun enters the sign of Aries, and indeed several thousand years ago when astrology was invented this was the case. But Earth's spin has a wobble, called precession of the equinoxes, and today when the sun is on the equator in spring it is in the constellation Pisces. Curiously, this slow drift of the equinox among the stars makes no difference to astrologers; they go on casting their horoscopes as if the sun were in Aries. And indeed it makes little difference to the rest of us. Earth tips toward the sun, leaning into its curve, soaking up energy from the core of the sun, animating the planet.

I've been reading Thoreau's journals, following him day by day as we approach the equinox. Here are extracts from his entries for 1858:

> March 14: I have seen many more tracks of skunks within two or three weeks than all the winter before; as if they were partially dormant here in the winter, and came out very early.

> March 16: A thick mist, spiriting away the snow. . . . This fog is one of the first decidedly spring signs; also the withered grass bedewed by it and wetting my feet . . . I walk in muddy fields, hearing the tinkling of newborn rills.

March 17: [Walk] to the hill. The air is full of bluebirds.
I hear them far and near on all sides of the hill, warbling
in the tree-tops . . . Ah! there is the note of the first flicker,
a prolonged, monotonous *wick-wick-wick-wick-wick-wick*,
etc. . . . This note really *quickens* what was dead. It seems
to put a life into withered grass and leaves and bare
twigs, and henceforth the days shall not be as they have
been.

March 18: The rather warm but strong wind now roars in
the wood — as in the maple swamp — with a novel sound.
I doubt if the same is ever heard in the winter. It apparently comes at this season, not only to dry the earth but to
wake up the trees, as it were, as one would awake a sleeping man with a smart shake.

March 19: To Hill and Grackle Swamp . . . I see little
swarms of those fine fuzzy gnats in the air . . . It is their
wings which are most conspicuous, when they are in the
sun . . . They people a portion of the otherwise vacant air.

March 20: We cross the Depot Field, which is fast becoming dry and hard. At Hubbard's wall, how handsome
the willow catkins! . . . Talk about a revival of religion!
. . . All Nature *revives* at this season . . . If a man do not
revive with nature in the spring, how shall he revive
when a white-collared priest prays for him?

Rebirth, waking up, revival: a common theme in the
writings of Thoreau. I follow his spirit, listening, watching.
We have more skunks in our neighborhood than previously,
more bluebirds, too, although nothing like the numbers
recorded by Thoreau. The *wick-wick-wick-wick-wick-wick* of
the flicker enlivens our woods, too. Their biological clocks

tick a daily and annual rhythm. "We must learn to reawaken and keep ourselves awake," wrote Thoreau, "not by mechanical means, but by an infinite expectation of the dawn." Staying awake. Redwings, meadowlarks, tree swallows, and bluebirds chant their lessons of where we have come from, where we have been, binding us up with all of nature in a constant reiteration of ancient themes, the perfecting machinery of eons of evolution, keeping us connected to the tap root of the soul.

As I write, I have in front of me an icon of the soul's evolution. He stands in a corner of my study, staring blankly. Again and again, I lift my eyes to see him. I call him Nari. I've grown quite fond of him. He is eleven or twelve years old, a strapping youth of about five feet three inches. He would have stood over six feet tall had he lived to maturity. He has been dead for 1.5 million years.

Nari is a poster boy. His image graces a poster supplied by Harvard University Press to advertise a book, *The Nariokotome Homo erectus Skeleton*, edited by Alan Walker and Richard Leakey. It is a handsome, haunting poster. Nari's life-size, almost complete skeleton is posed against a black background. The bones glisten with a rich bronze patina. To my untutored eye, the skeleton looks remarkably modern. The proportions of the body are graceful, almost delicate. I need only close my eyes and the fleshed-out boy steps forward, grinning good-naturedly, hand extended in greeting. Inspired by the poster, I obtained a copy of the book. I wanted to know more about Nari, about his life and death. I wanted to know how it is that the human soul came into existence, all those eons ago in the East African savanna. Not that I expected much in the way of answers. After all, how much is it possible to know about a boy who lived and died more than a million years before I was born? A surprising amount, it turns out. For one thing, Nari is the most complete early hominid (human ancestor) skeleton ever discovered. For another, his bones are among the most intensely studied fossils of all time. Walker and Leakey's book brings together contributions by experts in paleobiology, geology, anatomy, anthropology, and ecology. It is a stunning detective story and a satisfying demonstration of the power of the scientific method to flesh out the past.

The experts call him the Nariokotome boy, after the dry riverbed in northern Kenya near which he was discovered in 1984. His technical designation is KNM-WT 15000, the acquisition number of his skeleton at the Kenya National Museum. But I shall call him Nari, because that is how I have known him during the weeks he has occupied the corner of my study. Nari lived in rich grasslands bordering a river that flowed near what is the present basin of Lake Turkana. The river's seasonal flood left several large swamps that would take most of the year to dry out. The grasslands and swamps were home to many species of plant-eating animals, together with their attendant predators and scavengers. Volcanoes occasionally showered the river valley with blankets of ash. All of this information is pieced together from fossil and geologic clues.

How did Nari die? His skeleton shows no signs of violence. The only abnormal feature is an indentation in the jaw caused by inflammatory gum disease related to the loss of a tooth not long before his death. Before the advent of antibiotics, half a century ago, death from septicemia caused by abscessed teeth and gums was common. Perhaps Nari died from infection after shedding a milk tooth. At death, his body either fell into a swamp or was washed into it by a minor flood. For a while it floated facedown as it decomposed. The body drifted a few meters, was trod upon by hippos, sucked on by catfish, and chewed on by turtles. In time, nearly all of the bones came to rest in a shallow part of the swamp, became embedded in mud, and remained there for a million and a half years until they began to be eroded out of sediments at the side of a small tributary of the Nariokotome River.

In life, Nari was powerfully muscled, yet slender — a runner's build. He was at the age when he was perhaps learning the arts of hunting and gathering from his elders. Like them, he almost certainly prepared his prey for eating with carefully crafted stone choppers and scrapers. He probably used fire. All of this marks Nari as a true human ancestor. But there is so much more that we want to know, about which the bones are silent. Did Nari speak? Did he fall in love? Did he grieve for a dead friend? Did he dream? Did he look with wonder into the dark abyss of night? Did he gasp with delight at a green flash in the rising sun? Did he listen with knowing wonder to the song of returning birds in the vestibule of the season? The authors of *The Nariokotome Homo erectus Skeleton* struggle valiantly with the clues that might enable us to answer these questions. They measure the bones in every possible way, comparing them with modern skeletons. They examine the shape and size of the brain case, looking for clues to those parts of the brain known to be crucial for speech. They examine the air passageways of the nose and throat. They probe the spinal column for clues to the central nervous system. Four hundred pages of graphs, charts, schematics, measurements, and comparisons. In the end, the bones do not reveal their most precious secret: Nari's inner life.

I look again at the life-size poster. What was Nari thinking as he lay at the edge of the swamp, racked by the pain of infection, burning with fever? Did he know that he was going to die? Did he grieve for the life he would not live? Did he cry out at the unfairness of a universe that would take a boy in the prime of his life? If a skull can be said to have an expression, there seems to be a fierceness to Nari's face, perhaps even anger. Did he rage against the dying of the light with a fully human consciousness? Or was he silent, thoughtless, not yet capable of having or giving expression to thoughts of the terrible and the sublime? I can't tell you why, but looking at Nari's skeleton, I know that he is me—my bone, my blood, my dreams, my soul, rooted deep in the evolving mystery of self, long ago and far away.

Our four-footed ancestors kept their noses to the ground in search of food or mates, or watching out for enemies. At some point, they rose onto their hind legs and that at least got their eyes pointed at the horizon. When some bipedal, erect primate—perhaps of Nari's generation— tipped his head back and looked up at the sky, admired the stars, cocked his ear to birdsong, he became fully human, struck by beauty, humbled by depth, suffused with wonder.

On the day of the spring equinox in 1858, Thoreau wrote in his journal: "We need to see the honest and naked life here and there protruding." With Nari, or someone like him, our species wakened to honest and naked life. Our work now is to stay awake — in infinite expectation of the dawn.

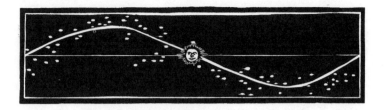

Vernal Equinox

 New Moon

Almost exactly a month after the redwings establish their song-bounded territories, as if called forth by the Earth's own equinoctial clock, the spring peepers are in full fortissimo chorus. On Nantucket they call these noisy little frogs pinkletinks, presumably because that's how Nantucketers hear the sound. I'm not sure how I'd describe the peeper's call. *Pinkletink* doesn't do justice to the volume. Not *peep-peep* either. The peeper's voice is shrill and high pitched, and when the water meadow is in heady voice it's like a zillion wedding guests clanking on glassware with spoons.

The peeper is only an inch long, but it's all voice box from stem to stern. Most frogs call by inflating air sacs under their chins; peepers inflate their entire bodies. The air is not completely expelled with each peep. The peeper uses its body like a bagpiper's bag, keeps it pumped up for the duration of its amatory calls. I stand by the side of the water meadow and the whole place seems to sing. You'd

swear they are everywhere; a carpet of sound stretches
away from my feet. But not a peeper in sight. I scan the
water with binoculars. The weeds and the bushes. Nary a
sign of the elusive frogs. Pure disembodied pandemonium.
The water itself seems to be emitting the noise. Off with the
shoes. Roll up the trousers. Into the water. Out to the very
middle of the water meadow. Suddenly, silence. As if someone has pulled the plug on the amplifier. I stand as still as a
statue. Five minutes, ten. Then, it starts up again, the ear-
splitting carpet of sound. The peepers are still invisible.

It's the male frog making all the noise, and we know
why. It's that old spring business all over again: finding a
mate. But why the tumultuous decibels? Why the din? We
are not talking about establishing territory—at least I
don't think so. Is the female peeper stone-deaf? Does she
choose a mate by the amplitude of his call? Has evolution
cranked up the volume of this chorus by finding a connec-
tion between the loudness of the love song and reproductive fitness? Or is it something else, something you won't
find in any biology book—pure excess vitality, a capacity
of water and muck to make noise, to celebrate? Of course
I'm being facetious, but not altogether so. I'm talking
about the astounding resiliency of life, its ability to survive
the harshest conditions and to spring up in the unlikeliest
places. The Roman naturalist Pliny the Elder wondered
about all those frogs coming out of nowhere in the spring
with their outrageous racket, and he attributed it to an "occult operation" of nature. In other words, magic. Sleight of
hand. Hocus-pocus. We are today more hardheaded about
it. We know the peepers have been there all along, buried

in the mud throughout the long winter, waiting for a couple of warm days to beckon them up into song. But what about life itself? What "occult operation" conjured life on Earth nearly four billion years ago out of water and muck? One minute the planet was lifeless (presumably), and the next minute (give or take a few tens of millions of years) the place was swimming with microbes. It's been swimming ever since.

Most biologists believe that life began spontaneously from nonliving materials. Charles Darwin imagined that it happened in a "warm little pond" somewhere on the early Earth, the quietly simmering primeval soup so dear to generations of biologists. According to this theory, chemicals stewing in water formed themselves into proteins, RNA, DNA, and ultimately the first living cells. But Darwin's warm little pond may never have existed. Recently, planetary scientists have been telling us that the Earth was a very nasty place at about the time life was beginning. The surface of the planet was subject to rampant volcanism. Meteorites rained from the sky for hundreds of millions of years, splattering the surface, the same incessant bombardment that cratered the surface of the moon (on Earth, the evidence of that early bombardment has been erased by erosion and tectonic activity). A few of the meteorites may have carried enough energy to completely vaporize the oceans. It's hard to image how or where in the midst of such chaos the complex and delicate structures of life were created and sustained. Perhaps it happened near volcanic fissures on the floors of the deepest oceans as the meteorites poured down. Perhaps in hot springs on continents as the bombardment waned. Or perhaps it happened deep, deep inside the rocky crust itself.

Since no one knows how life began, I'll opt for the theory that it was all inevitable. Start with a hydrogen-rich environment, throw in some carbon, expose it to energy, and — you've got amino acids, phosphates, sugars, and organic bases, the chemical building blocks of life (we can do this in the laboratory). Add cycles of heat and cold, dry and wet, light and dark, maybe a catalyst like iron pyrites or clay, and any old planet with a reasonably moderate environment might pull the rabbit out of the hat — or peepers out of the muck. I can't prove it, but I believe that water and mud have a built-in tendency toward animation, that life and soul are ubiquitous, not only here but throughout the universe. I don't mean to sound mystical, but if we've learned anything in the twentieth century it is that matter, plain old matter, is subtle stuff, prone to complexification, rich in infinite possibilities of combination. Just listen to that racket rising from the water meadow. That's what the spring peeper's hallelujah chorus is all about: the sheer, unstoppable ebullience of life.

 First Quarter Moon

"I have that haunting feeling that spring this year again performed all her old tricks and showed me just how life is made and what it is made of, but her hand has such sleight and she so distracts the attention with the waving green scarves and birds let loose from the loft that just when you think it is time now to watch carefully, the thing is done." So observed the American nature writer Donald Culross Peattie in *Green Laurels: The Lives and Achievements of the Great Naturalists*. He might have been talking about our New England spring, which for all the pinkletink hocus-pocus mostly isn't, until one day it was, and you wonder how you missed it. This year, as every year, we were treated to the usual diversions performed by the prestidigitator to tease us into misdirected attention. The skunk cabbage. The *conk-a-ree* of the redwings. The silky buds of the pussy willow. The peepers' chorus. We slip to the edge of our seats, waiting to catch the magician at her old trick, and then — presto! — the thing is done, finished, over. The rabbit is out of the hat and we have somehow been magically transported into summer.

In his meditation about spring, Peattie was writing about Jean-Henri Fabre, the French entomologist who devoted his life to the study of insects and their near relations. Fabre spent much of his life lying in ditches or crouched in the grass, peering in on the private lives of spiders, caterpillars, beetles, and ants. Of all the great naturalists chronicled by Peattie, Fabre spent his life closest to the ground. Forget the skunk cabbages, redwings, pussy willows and chorusing frogs. Insects make up more than half of all living things on the planet. In North America there are one hundred times more species of insects than species of birds, three times more species of insects than all plant species put together. How can spring happen and that multitude of six-legged creatures remain invisible? Of all the early spring insects, only the mourning cloak butterflies are conspicuous. They flag themselves before our eyes like bright silks plucked from the magician's sleeve. Some years, the mourning cloaks appear as early as February or March, roused from hibernation by a freak day of soaring temperatures (no preset circadian alarm clock for the mourning cloaks; their wake-up call is temperature). Almost uniquely among butterflies, mourning cloaks overwinter as adults, sleeping in protected nooks and crannies, until the first spring day with temperatures in the high fifties brings them flapping into the sun. And what distracting things they are, with handkerchief wings of purple-brown already fringed with summer's gold.

Water striders and whirligig beetles also overwinter as adults, which means they are out and about in early spring, although rather inconspicuous by comparison with mourning cloaks. There is a plank bridge not far from my house across a sluggish stream where it is pleasant to lie on one's belly during a warm spring afternoon and watch the stream come to life. The momentum of the stream's surface builds day by day, from icy inactivity to total frenzy, with slow, observable steps. There is no illusionist leap here from winter to summer; the surface of the stream is one place where nature's hand is *not* quicker than the eye. Spittlebugs, leaf beetles, tent caterpillars, solitary bees: these too are out early to catch the first saps and nectars of the season. Their increase is slow and steady, unlike the sudden jolt of the thermometer from the thirties to the seventies that deludes us into thinking that spring didn't happen. Insects give voice to the steady *tick-tock* of the New England spring. One thing follows another. No butterflies until sap is flowing at broken twigs. No spiderwebs until there are winged insects to snare. No caterpillars hatch from eggs until there are young leaves to munch. No nestlings in the robin's nest until the first big hatch of insect grubs. Watch. Watch. Pay attention. Stay awake. Don't be distracted by the gaudy scarves flashed conspicuously from nature's sleeves and birds let loose from lofts. Watch, watch nature's prestidigitating hand and see each incremental sleight by which she conjures a season.

Jean-Henri Fabre lived for spring. He had no other ambition than to chronicle the lives of insects; winter sent most of his beloved creatures to their nests, burrows, and rock-hard egg cases. For much of his life, Fabre worked as a schoolmaster or professor, for a meager salary that enjoyed no increase in twenty years. When his popular writing about insects at last began to produce a small, steady income, he bought a scraggly plot of land suitable only for spiders, scorpions, thistles, and himself. There he hunkered down among the weeds and watched insects in their element. At the end of a long life of impoverished anonymity he was lifted from obscurity and hailed as the "Homer of insects." He welcomed spring for the signs and signals we seldom notice—the hum, flitter, and skitter of ten thousand tiny creatures winding up into activity, teaching us with subtly increasing pressure how life is made and what it is made of—the hum, flitter, and skitter of nature's magic caught in the act.

◯ Full Moon — Grass Moon

And what do we see, down on our knees, nose in the grass? A thrips maybe. According to a story in the newspaper, Vermont maple syrup producers have been worried about the pear "thrip." According to the report, this little insect defoliates maple trees, which is not good for the sap.

First, let's get one thing straight. The newspaper notwithstanding, there's no such thing as *a thrip*. The singular of thrips is thrips. The plural of thrips is thrips. As Dr. Seuss might say, "One thrips, two thrips, red thrips, blue thrips." But then again, the thrips that afflict maples are neither red nor blue, but blackish or whitish, depending on the stage of their life cycle. Dark adult thrips spend the winter underground, emerging in the early spring to feed on buds, blossoms, leaves, and young fruits of various trees, including pears and sugar maples. They deposit eggs in leafstalks. Pale young thrips emerge from the eggs, eat, get fat, then fall to the ground, where they take up residence in the soil and lie dormant all summer. Transformation to the adult stage takes place in late fall, whereupon thrips then go to sleep for the winter. A simple life, mostly spent snoozing, by an almost invisibly small insect with a Dr. Seuss sort of name.

One of my favorite pastimes, in season, is to plunk a wildflower or weed onto the stage of a dissecting microscope and go exploring. No Darwin in the Galápagos or Humboldt on the Amazon ever surveyed a richer fauna than what exists microscopically on almost any plant. A dandelion can be a tropical forest for the naturalist armed with even a modest degree of optical magnification. Within the stamens and corollas of every meadow weed lurks an astonishing catalog of beasts, and among them are likely to be a few thrips. Now I wouldn't know a pear thrips from a wheat thrips or any other kind of thrips (there are hundreds), but I know a thrips when I see one. Adult thrips have four fringed wings, like tiny oars with eyelashes, and often I've found one skulking about in a flowerhead. Magnified ten times, even the wimpishly named thrips presents a formidable aspect. Eye to eye with one of these optically enlarged monsters, one can begin to understand how a thriving throng of thrips could thrash a maple.

No sooner had I read about thrips in Vermont than I came across another thrips story in the science journal *Nature.* "Facultative Viviparity in a Thrips," it was called, by Bernard Crespi of the University of Michigan. Crespi has discovered a species of thrips in which females lay eggs (oviparity) or give birth live (viviparity), or both. Oviparous offspring are female, and viviparous offspring are male. During a given bout of reproduction, it's all one way or the other, but long-lived females can change modes, and somehow the sex ratio balances out. Crespi's switch-hitting female thrips are apparently the only known animal capable of "choosing" her mode of reproduction in response to subtle signals from within or without. Curiosities like this are the delight of evolutionists. How and why did such bizarre behavior evolve? What is the adaptive value of being able to switch reproductive modes? Crespi posits plausible explanations, but an explanation by natural selection may be redundant. Thrips run the gamut of reproductive strategies. Some lay eggs, some give live birth, and one, at least— Crespi's thrips—has it both ways. *One fish, two fish, red fish, blue fish. A fish with a long curly nose. A fish like a rooster that crows. A fish with a checkerboard belly. A fish made of strawberry jelly.* Is it Dr. Seuss or reality? Nature seems to have a niche for almost everything. Not even the wildest product of the good doctor's imagination—the Moth-Watching Sneth, for example, a bird so big it scares people to death, or the Grickily Gractus that lays eggs on a cactus—is stranger than creatures that actually exist. I once mentioned these two mythical creatures in something I wrote for the *Boston Globe;* one reader sent me a photograph of a certain tropical bird that does indeed lay eggs on a cactus, and another reminded me of the extinct elephant bird of Madagascar, which stood ten feet tall, weighed a thousand pounds, and probably did scare many a Madagascan half to death. The egg-laying/ live-birthing Flip-Flop Thrips might have been invented by Dr. Seuss for our entertainment and delight. So, too, the Syrup-Sipping Thrips of Vermont. The naturalist Donald Culross Peattie wrote, "The world, from a weevily point of view, seems to exist for weevils." He might as well have said that the world from a human point of view seems to exist for humans.

Why does a biologist like Crespi spend all that time with nylon-mesh bags filled with dead oak leaves and live thrips, counting offspring, sexing baby thrips, and determining reproductive modes? OK, some thrips are agricultural pests, and one could argue—especially when applying for research grants—that studying the reproductive behaviors of thrips might have an economic payoff in pest control. But I doubt if such practical concerns have much to do with Crespi's motivation. If he is like other biologists I know, he is doing what he does for the same reason I go exploring with my microscope: he is following his curiosity into the bizarre Dr. Seussian world of biological diversity. There are more than ten million species of life on this planet, and we are the only one insatiably curious about all the rest. If somewhere there is a bird that lays eggs on a cactus, we want to know about it. If there once was a bird as big as an elephant, we are off to Madagascar to dig up the fossils. Not even the lowly thrips escapes our interest. Paying attention is what makes us human.

 Last Quarter Moon

In a posthumously published essay, Virginia Woolf wrote about special "moments of being" that sometimes interrupt the gray nondescript "cotton wool" of everyday life. One of those moments happened as she was looking at a flower in a garden at St. Ives. It was an ordinary plant with a spread of fine green leaves. She looked at the flower and said, "That is the whole." It had suddenly occurred to her that the flower was part of the Earth, part of everything else that was. The realization came as a hammer blow, she said, and from it emerged a philosophy: behind the quotidian cotton wool is hidden a pattern. The whole world is a work of art and we are part of it. It would be easy to dismiss this revelation as so much sentimentality, but Woolf was not a sentimental person. Many of her so-called moments of being brought with them a peculiar horror. For her, the recognition that we are at one with the world was a source of both exhilaration and despair. The world, after all, is both beautiful and terrible, creative and destructive, ordered and chaotic. Woolf's interest in the connectedness of things was not that of the sentimentalist, nor of the mystic, but of the writer. "We are the words," she wrote, describing the experience of the flower. "We are the music; we are the thing itself."

The scientist is no less sensitive than the writer to the connectedness of things, to the hidden patterns behind the cotton wool. But in practice, science works by *breaking connections*, by isolating, by fracturing the world into myriad parts like a shattered crystal ball. The laboratory bench is an arena for isolating one thing from another. An experiment is an attempt to reduce the many variables of experience to two—the dependent and the independent. This shattering of the world into fragments has proved fantastically successful as a way of discovering hidden patterns. We call this program "reductionism," by which we mean the reduction of experience to isolated, or *almost* isolated, elements. Once we have discovered the hidden patterns, then we attempt to weave the world back again into wholeness. However, what the public generally sees of science is the shattering, not the weaving into wholeness. They are properly suspicious of a method that focuses our attention on bits and pieces. As a species, we value wholeness. We thrive on those moments of being when we sense the connectedness of things. "Wholeness," wrote Woolf, "means that [experience] has lost its power to hurt me."

Most people realize that our health and economic well-being rely in large measure upon scientific knowledge of the world. At the same time, they distrust science. They find it abstract, incomprehensible, and remote from experience, especially remote from those rare epiphanies when we glimpse something whole and entire. They think of science the same way they think of the repair manual for an automobile or the schematic diagram for a piece of electronic equipment—of interest to the mechanics or electricians who keep our automobiles or television sets running, but boring for the rest of us. Of what relevance are cams or capacitors to the rush of a Ferrari when the stoplight changes from red to green, or to the excitement of the Superbowl viewed on a thirty-six-inch Sony?

But for the naturalist, an owner's manual to the world is everything. Without detailed, scientific knowledge of the way the world works, most of the world's stories remain untold. Knowledge lets nature speak. Here, pinned over my desk, is the cover of the June 23, 1989, issue of *Science,* tattered, faded with age. It is a photograph of a garnet crystal, in real life about the size of a bottle cap but here enlarged to fill the page, shaped like a paisley swirl—like the yang-yin symbol of Chinese philosophy. The crystal is embedded in a matrix of ancient metamorphosed granite broken from a mountainside in Vermont. The garnet crystal is a fragment that contains in miniature the history of the mountain itself—indeed, the history of the continent.

Geologists John Christensen, John Rosenfeld, and Donald DePaolo of the University of California discovered the crystal on a mountainside, where it had been exposed by eons of erosion. They sliced the crystal into thin segments and used radioactivity to measure the ages of the segments along the sweep of the yang-yin swirl. According to their measurements, the crystal grew at a rate of about 1.7 millimeters per million years for ten million years. All of this happened deep inside the Earth as the ancestral Green Mountains of Vermont were thrust upward. At that time, the drifting continents of northern Europe and Africa were approaching North America from the south (the resulting collision would create the supercontinent geologists call Pangaea). The squeeze of slowly converging continents folded the rocks of Vermont into an S-shaped loop called a nappe (from the French for "tablecloth"). Meanwhile, the garnet crystal was growing from a reservoir of molten minerals deep inside the crust, adapting its shape to stresses in the rock. The yang-yin shape of the crystal is a miniature image of what was happening to the mountains themselves.

The ancient mountains of New England with their looping tablecloth folds are now almost gone, erased by erosion. The surviving garnet crystal enables geologists to deduce the rate at which those mountains were heaved upward, stretched, folded, and implanted with granite. The crystal is a miniature record of ten million years of continental collision and mountain building—ten million years of the geologic history of New England. It is not quite William Blake's universe in a grain of sand, but close to it. It is part of the way the world is made that the whole is often contained in the part; upon that, at least, mystics and scientists agree. That's why reductionism works, why we can discern in fragments something of the weft and warp that binds the whole. When I first saw that photograph of the garnet crystal on the cover of *Science,* I experienced a kind of "moment of being." I vividly imagined the heavings and foldings of mountains that I had previously only read about. I looked at the photograph and I said, "That is the whole."

 New Moon

In the summer of 1868, the British Association for the Advancement of Science held its annual meeting in the town of Norwich, ninety miles northeast of London. At that meeting, Thomas Henry Huxley, one of the greatest natural historians of his day and a champion of Darwin's new theory of evolution by natural selection, delivered a talk titled "On a Piece of Chalk." His audience were the ordinary workingmen of the town. Huxley's subject was engagingly simple—and familiar. Some of the carpenters in the audience may have carried a piece of Norwich chalk in their pockets. The town is built upon chalk, the same extensive beds of soft, white rock that give England its poetic name—Albion (from the Latin *albus,* "white"). From a piece of Norwich chalk, Huxley extracted an astonishing story of a vast saltwater sea that once lay upon Britain and of the microscopic creatures that lived in the sea in prodigious numbers. In their dying, these tiny animals contributed their calcareous skeletons to bottom sediments that were ultimately compacted into chalk. The skeletons, of a wonderful geometric complexity, were often beautifully preserved in the chalk.

Eleven years earlier, the British Admiralty had commissioned Huxley's friend, a Captain Dayman, to sound the floor of the Atlantic Ocean along the route of the proposed transatlantic telegraph cable. Dayman sailed from Valentia, Ireland, to Trinity Bay in Newfoundland, measuring the depth of the sea and retrieving samples of mud from the ocean bottom. These specimens of deep-sea sediments were submitted to Huxley for examination. Huxley assured his Norwich audience that the sediments brought up from the floor of the present ocean contained exactly the same sorts of microscopic organisms that were preserved in the Norwich chalk. Where you saw the same effect, he said, you must assume the same cause. If the fossils in the Norwich chalk resembled in every respect the creatures found in the muddy depths of the present ocean—and nowhere else in the world—then it was reasonable to assume that the chalk was once sea-bottom sediments. The chalk beds at Norwich are hundreds of feet thick. "I think you will agree," Huxley told his audience, "that it must have taken some time for the skeletons of animalcules of a hundredth of an inch in diameter to heap up such a mass as that." How long? Embedded within the chalk were the fossils of higher animals—corals, brachiopods, sea urchins and starfish, altogether more than three thousand distinct, identifiable species of aquatic animals—animals that are found today only in salt seas. Among these fossils were some curious combinations, for example, a coral-covered shellfish affixed to a sea urchin. Here was a hint to the age of the chalk sea, and Huxley unraveled the story for his audience. The sea urchin lived from youth to age on the seafloor, then died and lost its spines, which were carried away. The shellfish adhered to the bare shell, and grew and perished in its turn. Finally, coral-building organisms covered both shellfish and urchin, lived out their lives, and expired. And all of this unfolded before slowly accumulating sediments encased these creatures in an inch or two of chalky mud. With a bit of extrapolation, it was easy for Huxley to deduce that tens of thousands of years, at least, were required for the deposition of chalk beds hundreds of feet thick.

But Huxley's story of the great depths of time was not yet complete. Where the River Yare flows through Norwich it cuts down through sandy clays to expose the chalk. Because the clays lie above the chalk, they must have been deposited at a later time. Between the clay and the chalk there is a layer of vegetative matter, including the fossilized stumps of trees standing as they grew—fir trees with their fossilized cones and hazel bushes with their fossilized nuts. Clearly, the chalk must have been uplifted above the floor of the sea before forests could grow upon it. And a greater surprise! Among the bolls of the trees are the fossilized bones of elephants, rhinoceroses, hippopotamuses, and other wild beasts that roamed the ancient forest, animals now found only in warmer southern climates. And above the forest beds, interspersed within clays of a marine origin, are the fossils of walruses and other cold-water sea animals now found only in the icy waters of the north. Sea, land, sea, and land again! Dramatic changes in climate! What forces caused such giddy transformations? Huxley did not know and readily confessed his ignorance. But he knew that the evidence of the Norwich rocks "compels you to believe that the Earth, from the time of the chalk to the present day, has been the theatre of a series of changes as vast in their amount as they were slow in their progress."

How astonished must have been the members of the Workingmen's Association of Norwich to hear of this dramatic extension of the history of their town. How different was the story told by Huxley from the story they had learned at Sunday school, derived from a literal interpretation of Genesis. How many of them chose to believe in the grand events apparently recorded in the chalk and overlying clay? How many dismissed Huxley's story in favor of the cozier, more human-centered tale of the Scriptures? We have no way of knowing. Huxley's lecture "On a Piece of Chalk" has come down to us as a little classic of scientific exposition, as engaging and informative today as in 1868. It was delivered only a few years after the introduction of Darwin's theory, at a time when the evolutionary interpretation of the Earth's past was still highly controversial. Huxley did not talk down to his audience. He did not grind theological axes. He simply directed their attention to the rocks and let the rocks speak for themselves. From his piece of chalk Huxley extracted an epic tale of evolutionary events that any teacher who has ever held a piece of chalk might envy. He taught us, with elegant simplicity, how to let the Earth tell its own story of its past.

Every stone, every pebble, every grain of sand has a story to tell. The trick is to listen, to prepare oneself with the requisite knowledge, then listen. Recently, I listened to a story of stones. My stones spoke in words of one syllable. *Clank. Clank. Clank.* I was digging postholes for a patio fence. Five holes, each one foot in diameter and two feet deep. At least that was the plan. By the time I had finished, I had five holes big enough for swimming pools. Some of the rocks I had removed from the earth were the size of fists, some were the size of basketballs, and one at least was the size of a thirty-pound turkey. A job that should have taken an hour took all weekend. The moral of the story: don't dig postholes in New England. Why so many rocks? Take a closer look. These rocks aren't local. They don't match the bedrock of the area, which is a greenish volcanic rock. The rocks I dug from the ground were granitic, metamorphic, sedimentary. Some of them came from Concord, New Hampshire. Some of them came from Montpelier, Vermont. Some of them came from Canada. All of them were dumped here fifteen thousand years ago, at the end of the last Ice Age, as the glacier melted. As the glacier moved down from its center of accumulation in central Canada, it scraped the land clean, right down to bedrock. All of that eroded material it carried along, like a moving river of ice and rock. Then, when the climate warmed and the glacier retreated, it dumped its load of rock and grit where the ice melted. Fine sand and silt were mostly carried away by meltwater and deposited on what is now the floor of the Atlantic Ocean. Heavier rocks were left where they fell. Some of them in my backyard. I listen to their story. *Clank. Clank. Clank.*

Once, I followed a chunk of this glacial debris to its source. Not far from my home there is a little hill of the green volcanic rock. On top of the hill are a half dozen huge boulders of pink granite, some of them the size of trucks. I knew their source could not be very far away because of their size. If they had had their origin in New Hampshire or Vermont or Canada, they would have been ground to pebbles or powder by their long journey in the ice. I chipped a fragment from one of the boulders and started walking north, orienting myself by the scratches on exposed outcrops of bedrock, always moving in the direction from which the ice had come. About three miles away, on the south side of a hill in the next town, I came to an ragged outcrop of granite that under a magnifier exactly matched the boulders. This was the boulders' source. As the ice moved over the hill, it plucked truck-size chunks of granite from the downstream side of the hill and carried them to my town. With enough patience, I could do the same for every rock I pulled from my backyard postholes. Every rock would have a source somewhere back along the line of scratches.

Geologists call this mix of assorted pebbles and boulders till. No history of New England is complete until you've included till. Native Americans who lived in this region before the coming of Europeans practiced a kind of agriculture that mostly ignored the stones in the soil. They cleared a patch of forest by burning, then scraped together heaps of dirt and planted them with corn, beans, or squash, with maybe a fish head or two thrown in for fertilizer. When the fertility of the soil declined, another field was cleared and the process started over. Cultivation was by hoes of shell or bone. It was hardscrabble work, but it worked just fine. For farming in the European fashion, however, the burn-and-scrape method was not just fine. The first sound the Pilgrims heard in the New World was metal hitting stone. They stuck their spades into the ground to dig foundations for their houses. *Clank*. They whacked at the ground with hoes to plant vegetables. *Clank*. They drove crowbars into the ground to raise a stockade. *Clank*. *Clank* was the sound of the New World's glacial history resisting the European way of life. *Clank* was the sound of stones telling a story of the deep past.

Most of the so-called soil of New England is glacial till, and it had to be planted if the first colonists weren't going to starve. Clearing stones from a field big enough for plowing was not the work of a weekend or even of a year; it was the work of a lifetime. The omnipresent stone walls of New England are a record of backbreaking labor. To avoid the stones, the first settlers sought out the few areas of relatively rock-free soil, mostly along streams or on the floors of meltwater lakes that existed in lowland basins near the end of the Ice Age. Water flowing into these lakes from the melting ice carried fine powdered rock, which settled onto the lake bottoms, building up thick beds of sediments. The largest glacial lakes, called Lake Hitchcock and Lake Upham by geologists, filled the valley of the Connecticut River from Hartford, Connecticut, to St. Johnsbury, Vermont. Other smaller lakes had existed in Concord and Taunton, Massachusetts, near Concord, New Hampshire, and in the valleys of the Nashua and Sudbury Rivers.

These scattered patches of sediments are New England's only premier farmland. When these choice lowlands had been cleared and planted, farmers were forced onto stony till. It is said that New England hill farms were so stony that sheep needed sharp noses to graze between the rocks. But it was rocks or nothing. By the mid-nineteenth century, 75 to 80 percent of southern New England had been cleared for farming, and most of that was on soil as thick with rock as my backyard. Only a fool would farm on glacial till if an alternative existed. When less stony land opened up west of the Alleghenies in the early nineteenth century, New England farmers locked the doors of their houses, took a boat on the Erie Canal, and went west. Their farms reverted to woodland. Today, two-thirds of southern New England is wooded, more than at any time since the mid-nineteenth century. My town is about two-thirds wooded, but there isn't an acre of those woodlands that doesn't contain stone walls and cellar holes of vanished houses, indicating that at one time the whole place was farmed. I once dug fifteen postholes in the woods of my college campus to set up markers for a nature trail. One hole was on the site of a dried-up glacial pond and the digging was easy. Fourteen holes were in the glacial till of old fields and pastures, now wooded, and I gained a backbreaking impression of what it must have been like to farm in New England before the opening of the Erie Canal. As I dug, I listened to the stories that came from the soil. *Clank. Clank. Clank.*

First Quarter Moon

My daughter, a geologist, brought me a gift from her ex-
pedition to the high Himalayan Plateau: a gray, water-
smoothed stone, of a size that fills the hand with a
satisfying heft. It is a limestone cobble, polished in a mountain steam, a one-pound chunk of rock eroded from a
towering peak—perhaps Everest, the highest place on
Earth—transported by a glacier, tumbled by rushing
water, finally tossed upon a bank of rounded cobbles at the
side of a river in a remote Himalayan valley. The stone is
cracked. Its top lifts away like the lid of a jewel box.
Inside—a fossil ammonoid.

Ammonoids are sea creatures, now extinct, shelled rela-
tives of squids and octopuses, cousins of the chambered
nautilus. The typical ammonoid fossil shell looks like a
tightly spiraled ram's horn, ribbed with wavy corrugations.
From the Carboniferous to the Cretaceous periods of geologic history—350 to 65 million years ago—ammonoids
were among the most abundant ocean animals, evolving
thousands of species. Today, they dominate the fossil
record of those far-off times. The fossil in my stone is about
three inches in diameter. There are no residues of the animal's soft tissue—the bulging eyes or waving arms that
searched for food. Only the shell has left its imprint in the
rock. Still, the impression of life is vivid. When I first
opened the stone, it was as if I had disturbed the animal in a
deep geologic sleep. There is a poem by Charles Simic in

which the poet muses on what it is like to be a stone and—wonderfully—imagines the stone having an inside and an outside. The spirit of the stone resides in the cool dark interior, says Simic, in hermitlike repose. If the stone is thrown into a river, it "sinks, slow, unperturbed / To the river bottom / Where fishes come to knock on it / And listen." The poet might have been thinking of my stone, my limestone cobble, with its secret inner life, its curled creature. I knock and listen.

One hundred million years ago, an ammonoid lived in the sea that then separated India from Asia. It died and fell into limy sediments on the seafloor. These sediments grew deeper and hardened into rock. The shell calcified, becoming part of the rock, though maintaining every detail of its structure. India was on the move, drifting on a slab of the Earth's mobile crust toward Asia. The floor of the intervening sea was forced under the Asian continent, back into the hot interior of the planet. As it descended, some of the limestone sediments were scraped off and piled against the overlying continent. Meanwhile, about sixty-five million years ago, an asteroid smashed into the Earth, possibly near the tip of the present Yucatan Peninsula in Mexico. The place of impact was far from India and Asia, but the effects of the catastrophe were global. A vast quantity of dust was hurled into the atmosphere. Winds carried the dust worldwide, wrapping the planet in a dark shroud that sunlight could not penetrate. Temperatures fell. Photosynthesis ceased. Food chains collapsed. The calamity caused the dinosaurs to become extinct. But dinosaurs were not the only victims. Huge numbers of other plant and animal species perished, both on land and in the sea. Not least among them were the ammonoids. This wildly successful family of creatures disappeared from the Earth. Only in the rocks did their images survive. About fifty million years ago, the sea separating India and Asia was at last squeezed out of existence, and the continents collided. A double-thickness continent was heaved upward, creating the high Himalayan Plateau. Among the crumpled rocks of the plateau were scraped-off sediments from the vanished seafloor. Some of these fossiliferous limestones were lifted to the peaks of the highest mountains, miles above sea level. Throughout all of this violence, my ammonoid slept, secure in its stony dreams. The violent hand of crustal motion lifted the rock from out of its limy matrix, held it to its mountainous ear, shook it, and rattled it. Water caressed it, whispering questions. Fish came to knock and listen. The stone was silent, unperturbed.

In his poem, Simic wonders if the inside of a stone is dark. He has seen sparks fly out when two stones are struck together, he says, so perhaps there is a pale interior light, like the light of a moon shining from behind a hill: "Just enough light to make out / The strange writings, the star-charts / On the inner walls." I open my stone, my daughter's gift. Daylight floods the interior, after 100 million years of darkness. Here on the inner walls, even as the poet guessed, are strange fossilized writings, telling of waters teeming with many-tentacled swimmers, of drifting continents, of asteroids, of limestone mountains lifted from the floor of a sea. The sleep of eons disturbed. I listen. I knock upon my limestone cobble and listen. I hear a story of wholeness. Of connectedness. We are words of the story. We are the music of the Earth. We are part of the story, part of the stone. We are the thing itself.

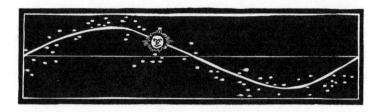

May Day

◯ Full Moon — Planting Moon

Why do killdeers build their nests on open ground? There are woods nearby, thickets, a field of rough boulders, all seemingly providing more security. Yet here is a killdeer nest on almost bare earth, among a scatter of twigs and stones. Which is not to say that the nest is obvious. Each day when I return to check the progress of the eggs, it takes me a few moments to find the brooding parent on her nest — and I know exactly where to look. Her brown, black, and white coloration blends perfectly with earth, twigs, and pebbles. When she leaves the nest (or is it he? the sexes are almost indistinguishable), the eggs themselves are even more difficult to see — speckled brown ovoids in a saucer of wood chips. The killdeers seem to act on the principle that less is more. If you are building a nest on open ground, then the nest itself should be inconspicuous — a shallow scrape, a few bits of debris. The birds do not choose their nesting site at random. They are driven by instinct to open ground. The architecture of the nest is likewise innate to the species, as much a part of the killdeer's genetic inheritance as the shape and color of the eggs.

Approach too closely and you are in for a show. The parent leaps from the nest and begins a frantic diversion, calling furiously (the bird's scientific name is *vociferus*), spreading its tail, flopping one wing as if it were broken, skittering about the ground, doing everything possible to distract the intruder—a bit of instinctive parental devotion that leaves one gasping with admiration. Approach more closely yet and the bird will scamper far from the nest, desperately trying to draw you away. Now, examine the eggs. A typical killdeer brood contains four eggs (this nest has three). Incubation takes twenty-four to twenty-eight days. If I want to see the nestlings, I had better be here when they hatch, because within an hour of so they are up and out of the nest, never to return. While brooding, the adult birds regularly turn the eggs to keep them evenly warm. Astonishingly, the eggs in the nest I have been watching are placed with pointy ends together, the most compact arrangement. This arrangement has been too rigorously maintained to be accidental; this behavior too is coded in the genes.

Inside each of the eggs is a growing embryo that has already been instructed on the business of arranging eggs with pointy ends together. Even as the killdeer's brain takes form, the impulse for the adult bird to turn pointy ends together is being wired into the circuitry. Let's go back a bit further, to the first microscopic fertilized cell that will become the embryo. In that cell are strands of DNA. The DNA molecule is shaped like a spiral staircase—the famous double helix. The side rails of the staircase are linked sugars and phosphates. The treads are paired molecules called nucleotides. There are four kinds of nucleotides: adenine, guanine, cytosine, and thymine, usually designated A, G, C, and T. Adenine always pairs with thymine, and guanine always pairs with cytosine, so that there are four kinds of treads along the DNA staircase: A-T, T-A, C-G, and G-C. It is the sequence of these treads that is the genetic code. Somewhere along the strand is a sequence of base pairs that will cause the adult birds to arrange eggs pointy ends together. We *know* it is true, yet it almost surpasses belief. All killdeer behaviors (circling flight, horizontal run, collar show, scraping, side tilt, bobbing), all killdeer auditory calls (*kideah* call, stutter call, *pup-pup* call), all killdeer characteristics of courting, feeding, parenting, and flocking are spelled out in a helical strand of DNA in the nucleus of a cell that is too small to be seen. I stand twenty feet away from the killdeer nest, with my Stokes bird guide in my pocket, staring through binoculars into the suspicious eyes of the brooding parent, and I am suddenly struck with the immense improbability of it all, the immense improbability of life. It is all chemistry, apparently. But not *only* chemistry. This is chemistry with a cosmic spark we have only begun to understand; this is chemistry with soul.

If you want to understand the chemistry of soul, it is best not to begin with a creature as complex as a killdeer, and certainly not with a creature as complex as a human. Nor should you begin with a single-celled organism, the bacterium *Escherichia coli*, for example. Rather, start with something complex enough to exhibit interesting behaviors and simple enough to be tractable. For example, start with the soil nematode *Caenorhabditis elegans,* the neurobiologist's favorite animal. Nematodes are threadlike worms. They range in length from a millimeter to a meter. A handful of rich loam might contain a thousand. They live virtually everywhere—soil, water, desert sand, arctic ice, hot springs, and as parasites of plants and animals. Pinworms and hookworms, familiar parasites of humans, are nematodes. The American parasitologist N. A. Cobb once asked us to imagine everything in the world suddenly disappearing—animals, plants, air, water, soil, the rocky body of the Earth itself—everything except nematodes. The world would still be recognizable, he said, as a ghostly hollow sphere of worms. Mountains, valleys, rivers, ponds, plants, and animals would still be distinguishable by the clouds of worms that used to inhabit them. From this vast host, *C. elegans* has been lifted from obscurity to scientific fame. This lowly nematode species has been chosen from a million nematode cousins to become one of the best-understood animals on Earth. I did an electronic search of the biological literature from 1988 to the present. Nearly eight hundred journal articles discussed *C. elegans.* This is far less than the bacterium *E. coli* with 21,594 entries, the all-time favorite subject of biological researchers, and not close to drosophila, the famous fruit fly of genetic experimenters, at 5,611 entries. But our little nematode is a rising star. "Some are born great, some achieve greatness, and some have greatness thrust upon 'em," says Malvolio in William Shakespeare's *Twelfth Night,* quoting Maria's letter. *C. elegans* has had greatness thrust upon it.

Why have these tiny worms, as thin as spider silk, as short as the diameter of a pinhead, been rocketed to fame? Their life cycle is quick, a three-day generation time, which is handy for genetic studies. They reproduce happily in the lab. They can be frozen for storage and revived as needed. Best of all, they are transparent; their insides are as easy to see as their outsides. And they are simple. They wriggle, eat, defecate: a life reduced to basics. They are mostly self-fertilizing, so they don't even need to bother looking for a mate. For these minimal activities, *C. elegans* requires a mere 959 body cells, including 302 neurons, no more, no less. The "parts list" of this tiny worm is about as long as that of your washing machine—and as exactly known. We know how *C. elegans* is put together, cell by cell, and even how the cells divide and differentiate from the single cell of the fertilized egg. The task now is to discover how the genes direct the construction of the worm. As a first step, scientists are trying to completely determine the "four-letter" DNA code that is the blueprint for making a nematode. *C. elegans* has approximately 100 million nucleotides in its DNA, compared to three billion nucleotides for humans. As I write, more than half of these have been determined; by the time you read this the task may be complete. Already it is clear that many of the nematode's genes appear to be closely related to certain human genes, including genes that cause diseases such as early-onset Alzheimer's and cystic fibrosis. Some of the worm's chemical machinery controlling neuron activity also appears to be similar to our own.

We are more closely related to the lowly worm than we might care to admit.

It won't be long before researchers have determined the complete genetic code of *C. elegans,* mapped the genes on the worm's six chromosomes, and linked genes to developmental features. Then little *C. elegans* will be as completely described as any multicelled animal—every nucleotide, every gene, every cell. Will that then be the end of the mystery of life? Not at all! It is only the beginning. The more we learn about the machinery of life, the more wonderfully miraculous it seems. *C. elegans* may have about as many cells as your washing machine has parts, but your washing machine doesn't start with one part (a gasket, say) and grow into a thousand parts (gaskets, drums, valves, dials, etc.). Your washing machine doesn't squirm, eat, and defecate. Your washing machine doesn't make other washing machines. Your washing machine doesn't colonize every habitat. We have more, much more to learn about the machinery of life. How do those DNA strands, which are snarls to start with, unwind and reproduce over and over without getting hopelessly tangled? How are errors in the DNA code corrected, at lightning-fast speed? How does a "one-dimensional" genetic code (a sequence of nucleotides) reliably build three-dimensional shapes—a worm, a killdeer, a human? How does a DNA molecule always find just the right chemical compounds it needs to reproduce itself—or make a protein? How do genes tell some cells to become gut and other cells to become muscles? How are complex behaviors such as arranging eggs with the pointy ends together chemically determined and expressed? How,

how, how? Some big surprises may be in store before we have answered all these questions. *C. elegans* may be one of the best-understood animals on Earth, but it is still a millimeter-long bundle of mystery.

 Last Quarter Moon

For the past several weeks tree swallows have been nesting in bluebird boxes on nearby conservation land. The boxes weren't meant for swallows, but, well, it's spring and first come, first served. What beautiful birds! Shimmering blue-green backs. White bellies. Strike-out speed. They zip and stitch the morning meadow, quicker than the eye can follow. Then, this past weekend, new boxes went up in the meadow. The next morning a pair of bluebirds was in residence, the first in these meadows in decades: blue-backed, robin-red-breasted, round-shouldered insect snatchers, flitting through the hedges or the branches of the pear trees. Who can see a bluebird and not be happy? The turn-of-the-century naturalist John Burroughs heard the bluebird's song as *pur-i-ty, pur-i-ty.* Other early naturalists heard *tru-al-ly, tru-al-ly.* No one with an ounce of sentimentality in his or her soul doubts that bluebirds are both pure and true.

There was a time when bluebirds were as common hereabouts as robins. Then, especially in the 1950s and 1960s, their numbers took a nosedive. A generation of New Englanders grew up without ever seeing one of these gentle, beautiful birds. The "bluebird of happiness" seemed a

mythical creature, invented by Judy Garland, living somewhere over the rainbow. What caused their decline? Bluebirds are hole-nesting birds; the replacement of wooden
fence posts with metal posts and the pruning of dead wood
from orchards eliminated many natural cavities, and starlings and house sparrows displaced bluebirds from the remaining nests. But a lack of nesting sites isn't the whole
story. Severe winters took their toll. Pesticides killed many
of the insects upon which bluebirds feed. And, of course,
the widespread use of DDT coincided with the bluebird's
most precipitous decline. Until their recent comeback, the
last bluebird I had seen in our town was in 1965, only three
years after the publication of Rachel Carson's *Silent Spring.*
Carson's book exposed the massive, indiscriminate use of
pesticides, especially DDT, and gloomily assessed the consequences for the environment. Those were days when
DDT was sprayed or dusted over half the landscape as a
weapon against Dutch elm disease, spruce bud worm,
gypsy moths, mosquitoes, and agricultural pests. The more
Carson looked into the use of chemical poisons, the more
alarmed she became. Her book was a brilliant, impassioned
call to arms against entrenched interests in government,
agriculture, and the chemical industry. It may be the most
influential book ever addressed to a popular audience by a
scientist. So successful was her rallying cry that within
months of the book's publication, many states and foreign
countries issued bans on DDT. In 1957, the U.S. Depart-
ment of Agriculture sprayed nearly five million acres with
DDT; in 1968, the figure had dropped to zero. The role of
chemicals in the bluebird's decline has been hotly debated,

but insect-eating birds are easy victims of pesticides. What a pleasure, then, to see a new pair of bluebirds take up residence in our meadow. Male and female, they perch on the roof of their box and survey the world, the essence of quiet domesticity. "Pur-i-ty, pur-i-ty," they seem to call. "Tru-al-ly, tru-al-ly," I silently answer.

The tree swallows will not leave them alone. Diving and darting, the swallows harass the bluebirds, send them fluttering from their box, shattering their repose. New metaphors for the swallows came to mind. Their backs are slick, Brylcreme blue. They dart with zip-gun speed. They fling themselves into the air like sky-smart, speed-crazed teenage hoodlums looking for trouble. The hapless bluebirds are innocent victims. Wait a minute! What is this compulsion to anthropomorphize the birds? Why am I so emotionally caught up in their drama? Why can't I just let the swallows and bluebirds be? It's an old habit, deeply ingrained in our race, to see ourselves in the animals. Aesop did it. Philosophers and theologians of the Middle Ages did it. Nineteenth-century naturalists did it, and the tradition carried over into our own century. Here is the American nature writer Neltje Blanchan describing the house wren, in a book that educated and entertained my grandparents: "If you fancy that Jenny Wren, who is patiently sitting on the little pinkish chocolate-spotted eggs in the center of her feather bed, is a demure, angelic creature, you have never seen her attack the sparrow, nearly twice her size, that dares put his impudent head inside her door. Oh, how she flies at him! How she chatters and scolds! What a plucky little shrew she is, after all!" In another bird handbook from early in the century, Mabel Osgood Wright describes the American crow as a "feathered Uriah Heep" and the jay as a "robber baron." The bluebird is the "color-bearer of the spring brigade" and the song sparrow is "the bugler." One enchanting bit of bird anthropomorphizing is F. Schuyler Mathews's description of the meadowlark's song as the first two bars of Alfredo's aria in *La Traviata,* "sung with charming accuracy." Mathews was another of the ornithologists who instructed my grandparents.

That's all gone now. Anthropomorphic references in a nature handbook today would undermine the author's authoritativeness and credibility. Styles have changed. We no longer see ourselves in the animals. We are more likely to see signs of the animals in ourselves. So much DNA code is shared among us; nematodes, bluebirds, and humans have common chemistry. Sociobiologists look to our genetic affinity with other animals to explain not only our physical frame but also many of our moral and intellectual behaviors. Harvard's E. O. Wilson, the father of sociobiology, has written that "the brain exists because it promotes the survival and multiplication of the genes that direct its assembly. The human mind is a device for survival and reproduction, and reason is just one of its various techniques." Thus, we look into our brain stems for shadows of reptilian ancestors. We examine the anthill for the origins of human societies. We watch gorillas and chimps in the wild to discover the roots of human aggression and sexuality. Even our ethical systems and religions are influenced by our evolutionary heritage, say sociobiologists. It is not so much that the crow is a "feathered Uriah Heep" as that we are crows. It is not so much that jays are "robber barons" as that human robber barons share an aggressive acquisitiveness with jays. The telescope has been turned around and we look at animals through the other end of the instrument.

This inversion of viewpoint is one of the most significant intellectual developments of our time. It has profound implications for sociology, psychology, and biology. It changes the way we think about environmentalism, ecology, and animal experimentation, perhaps even how we eat. Philosophers and theologians are busy working out how our animal nature gives rise to soul, our sense of purpose, our ultimate destiny. Aesop and the sociobiologists share a conviction that our common cause with animals is more than limbs, brains, gullets, and genitals. For Aesop and medieval philosophers, animals symbolize human vices and virtues. For the sociobiologists, humans embody animal characteristics through the agency of genes and evolution. For most of us in the Disney generation, our imaginations are trapped somewhere between the two poles. My anger at the swallows for harassing the bluebirds, and the rush of anthropomorphic metaphors that came to mind, are indicative of my own split allegiances: I am a good scientific materialist with one foot firmly planted in the Aesopian ornithology of another era. I know about the value-free determinism of genes. But I listen to bluebirds, newly returned to our meadows, and I hear *pur-i-ty, pur-i-ty.*

New Moon

If you are an early-morning walker in late spring or early summer, and if your path takes you by sandy soil near a pond, and if the God of Reptiles is awake and taking care of business, then you are sure to come upon a snapping turtle laying eggs. And what a sight! This lumbering behemoth from the age of dinosaurs, this nightmare-ugly Mesozoic monster, this carapaced misanthrope, this—uh, oh, I'm getting carried away. Be still. Don't startle. She is in the midst of her preparations, spread-eagle on the sandy slope, her arrowlike tail pointed to the pond, using her hind legs to excavate a deep, flask-shaped hole. She's a good-size snapper, maybe a foot from stem to stern, a rough thing of leather and chitin. She sees me. She casts a wary eye in my direction, but goes on about her business. I creep as close as I can get and still focus my binoculars. And suddenly I feel abashed. There is something intimate, intensely private about this business of laying eggs. The binoculars add to my sense of being a pondside Peeping Tom. She has almost buried herself. I scramble down the pond bank to obtain a rear-end view. And now she lays. *Plop. Plop. Plop.* Twenty-two leathery white eggs, the size of plump grapes, eased carefully into the hole. A dinosaurian gum-ball machine disgorging its contents.

It is impossible to watch a snapping turtle lay without thinking of J. W. P. Jenks of Middleboro, Massachusetts. The story of Jenks's youthful adventure, "Turtle Eggs for Agassiz," recounted by nature writer Dallas Lore Sharp around 1910, was a classic for generations, often anthologized, but now, like other antiquated tales of pluck and patience, sadly out of fashion. It is worth retelling. At the age of twenty-three, John Whipple Potter Jenks was appointed principal of Middleboro's Pierce Academy. One day Louis Agassiz, Harvard professor of zoology and America's most famous scientist, appeared at the doorway of Jenks's classroom. The great man asked if the young teacher might supply him with turtle eggs for his study of turtles, part of his monumental four-volume *Contributions to the Natural History of the United States of America*. Jenks said yes. The catch was this: if the proper information was to be obtained by dissection, the turtle eggs could not be more than three hours old. The distance from the pond in Middleboro where Jenks hoped to find the eggs to Agassiz's home in Cambridge was forty miles. And thereby hangs the tale.

On May 14, well before turtles were likely to lay, Jenks began his morning vigils at the pond. There he sat, alone among the cedars, from 3 A.M. until the bell at the academy announced early classes. Here is how he described those mornings, many years later, to Dallas Lore Sharp: "What fragrant mornings those were! How fresh and new and unbreathed! The pond odors, the woods odors, the odors of the plowed fields—of water lily, and wild grape, and the dew laid soil! I can taste them yet, and hear them yet—the still, large sounds of the waking day—the pickerel breaking the quiet with his swirl; the kingfisher dropping anchor; the stir of feet and wings among the trees. And then the thought of the great book being held up for me!" As he waited, day after day, week after week, Jenks came to know individually the dozen or more turtles that kept to his side of the pond. But no eggs, at least not yet. He sat and watched, Sundays and rainy days included, until finally an enormous female snapper came shuffling up out of the pond. She paddled across the meadow to a sandy bank, excavated a nest, and laid her eggs. No sooner had she finished than Jenks scooped up her cache and layered them with sand into a bucket. It was 4 A.M. on a Sunday morning, and he had three hours to get his treasure to Cambridge. I'll only sketch the rest of the story: the wild gallop toward the Boston Pike, the unexpected freight train, the frenzied hackney ride across the Charles River, the knock on the door of Agassiz's house just as the clock struck seven, the distraught face of Agassiz's maid as she opened the door upon a disheveled young man with a bucket of sand. Sharp's account is well worth reading for the details. Suffice it to say that Jenks was acknowledged in the preface of "the great book."

Pluck and patience. Necessary virtues if one is going to watch turtles. No other creature so big moves and acts with such deliberation. *Plop. Plop.* Twenty-one. Twenty-two. Then the careful burial. The push and pat of the back feet. The swish of the tail, like a broom, disguising. A last suspicious glance at me. The shuffle and slide back into the pond. It is the snapper's deliberateness that sets her apart. And maybe that's why I feel abashed as I watch her lay. It is not a personal intimacy that I intrude upon, but the intimacy of another age, a slower, more patient age, an age

willing to wait for a month, or a hundred million years if
necessary, for something to happen.

 First Quarter Moon

Snapping turtles, of whatever age, bear an aura of antiq-
uity, the hoary demeanor of Methuselah. For the Ephemer-
optera, or mayflies, life is ephemeral. An adult mayfly lives
for minutes or hours. Most of their adult lives is spent in
nuptial flight. On warm evenings in late spring or early
summer, male mayflies launch themselves into the air in flit-
tery swarms, rising and falling. Each female that joins the
throng is promptly seized by a male. The couple leave the
swarm and mate. She lays her eggs and dies, together with
her paramour. A single evening is the mayfly's allotted time.
From the point of view of evolution, it's the perfect life: flit,
procreate, die. Turtles enjoy a more protracted span, in
keeping with their torpid ways. The longest authenticated
lifespan of any animal is that of "Marion's tortoise," taken
as an adult from its native Seychelles Islands to the island of
Mauritius by the French explorer Marion Du Fresne in
1766. This huge lumbering beast survived past 1918, for a
record age of more than 152 years.

Only turtles live longer than humans. We can outlive
two (successive) hippopotamuses, three cats, four dogs, or
seven aardvarks. Hippos and aardvarks seldom complete
their allotted span. Most often, they are struck down in the

prime of life by predators or disease. Death from old age is
an almost uniquely human privilege, shared only with our
pampered and protected pets. Even for us, the expectation
of a ripe old age is relatively new. Ninety years ago only one
American in two reached the age of sixty. Today, nine out of
ten survive for at least six decades. The survival curve, as
they say, is becoming more "rectangular." The ultimate goal
is for everyone to live with reasonable vigor for the maximum span of life, then —*kerplunk,* fall off the brink. And we
are doing it, too. More and more of us in the developed
countries enjoy an active, independent old age, thanks to
healthier diets and lifestyles, and modern medicine.

The survival curve of animals in the wild is anything but
rectangular. It begins to plunge from day one. For example,
lapwings (Old World birds related to plovers) have a maximum lifespan of about ten years, but only one bird in ten
makes it half that long. Nature is bloody red in tooth and
claw—so red that old age is the exception rather than the
rule for animals in the wild. For most of human history, our
survival curve was not much different from that of lapwings. A typical human lifespan was thirty or forty years
because of the prevalence of disease, violence, and accidents. Aging wasn't a worry because almost no one died
of old age. Now all of that has changed. Our species, and
our pets and domesticated animals, have escaped the four-
billion-year-old dynamic of evolution. We have dulled nature's teeth and trimmed her claws, and more than the
fittest survive. We are no longer content to flit, procreate,
and die; we want to be fit and active to the very threshold of

oblivion. That's what the "rectangular" survival curve is all about.

But why stop at the allotted three score years and ten? Why not push the maximum human lifetime further up the scale, to age 100, say, or 120, or—what the heck, what's to keep us from living forever? Scientists do not yet fully understand the cause or causes of aging, but the process appears to be at least partly controlled by genes that trigger physical decline—sometimes called gerontogenes. There are lots of credible theories to explain why gerontogenes evolved. The one I like best (for no particular scientific reason) proposes that these genes became embedded in our chromosomes because natural selection could not prevent them from doing so. For animals in the wild, few individuals lived long enough for the gerontogenes to kick in. According to this view, aging is a fluke, a genetic quirk that wasn't selected for or against because it didn't make any evolutionary difference. No one died of old age.

What next? Scientists have bred fruit flies that live twice as long as their ancestors, and robustly, too. No one has yet figured out how to do the same for humans (scientists can't selectively breed humans), but as we learn more about the causes of aging you can bet it will happen. Sometime early in the twenty-first century, genetic engineers will jigger the gerontogenes to give us longer lifespans, and biochemists will figure out how to delay or thwart the genes' effects. When the human survival curve is stretched out twice as long, we will displace the tortoise as the champion of longevity—and distance ourselves even more from the Darwinian perfection of mayflies. Not flit, procreate, and die—but flit, procreate, and flit, flit, flit.

 Full Moon—Flower Moon

Lady's slipper. Moccasin flower. Squirrel shoes. The scientific name for the plant is *Cypripedium,* which is Latin combined with Greek for "slipper of Venus." The early French explorers of North America called it *le sabot de la Vierge,* "the sabot of the Virgin" (a sabot is a wooden shoe worn by peasants in France). Try as I might, I cannot see a shoe or slipper in this plant. Perhaps, with a stretch of the imagination, the inflated hanging sac of the flower bears some resemblance to the wooden shoes of peasants I have seen in paintings by Vincent van Gogh. But no matter—the pink lady's slipper is New England's most spectacular wildflower, and spring is its season. The gaudy plant would appear more appropriate to a tropical forest or an orchid fancier's hothouse than to our discreet Yankee woodlands. It is irresistibly lovely, and in a less environment-conscious time it was in danger of being picked out of existence. "It is becoming rarer every year," says a wildflower guide published in 1917, "until the finding of one in the deep forest, where it must now hide, has become the event of a day's walk." The lady's slipper was once so rare in our area that it was considered an endangered species. In some states the flower is protected by law, but it is certainly no longer rare. In one piney woods near my home, the plants are so numerous that it is difficult to take a step without crushing one underfoot. Like the bluebird, the lady's slipper is making a comeback.

As a family, the orchids are generally successful: they include more species than any other family of plant. Most orchids are natives of the Tropics, but our pink lady's slipper may give us a clue to the family's success. It is ingeniously designed to compel pollination by insects — typically bees — and to guard against self-pollination. Self-pollination in plants produces a seed that is genetically almost identical to the parent. When the pollen of one plant makes its way to a different plant it is called cross-pollination. Cross-pollination mixes genes and makes it more likely that offspring will be different from parents. As Darwin was the first to note, cross-pollination may give rise to hardier species of plants that are better able to adapt to their environment. The blossom of the lady's slipper fairly forces cross-pollination. There are two ways for an insect to enter the flower: through the long, inward-curving slit at the front of the sac, or through two little holes at the top of the sac that are hidden by petals. Attracted by color or scent, the insect invariably enters at the front and soon discovers that it has passed through a one-way door into a voluminous chamber, lush with nectar but with no obvious exit. If the insect persists in its explorations, it will find its way toward the two escape holes at the top of the sac. Forcing its way upward through the narrow passage toward freedom, the insect first encounters the female part of the plant, the stigma, which is equipped with tiny bristles, like a lint brush. The brush removes from the body of the

bee whatever pollen it has carried from another lady's slipper. But escape is not yet complete. The bee struggles on
toward one of the small round exits, where a male part of
the plant, an anther, almost blocks its way. Forcing passage, the bee becomes covered with pollen. Free at last, it is
ready to pollinate whatever plant it visits next, although
one wonders why, after so much trouble, it has not learned
to leave well enough alone. There is no possibility, in this
system of one-way doors and passageways lined with
forward-pointing bristles, that the insect can get to the male
part of the flower before the female part. Self-pollination is
virtually ruled out by architecture. (I have read somewhere
that very large bumblebees sometimes find escape impossible through the flower's narrow pollen-retrieving/pollen-
supplying passages. A trapped bee has two alternatives:
to bite its way out through the side of the sac, or, as my
1917 guidebook says, "to perish miserably in its gorgeous
prison." I have looked into the gorgeous sacs of dozens of
lady's slippers hoping to find some poor bumblebee in-
terred, so far without success.) The blossom of the plant
might seem to be a mere extravagance of beauty, an orna-
ment, a flourish of ostentation. It is not. It is a highly perfected reproductive apparatus that has coevolved with the
bee. The blossom of the lady's slipper has one purpose—
making another blossom.

And what a process! Each plant begins life as a single
fertilized cell. One cell becomes two; two become four; four
become eight. As they split, the cells diversify for special
functions: root, stem, leaves, petals, corolla. The process is
called morphogenesis—the development of a complex,

multicelled organism from a fertilized egg. Aristotle thought
a creative spirit associated with the male sperm gave shape
to the amorphous material of the female egg. Other ancient
thinkers imagined that every germ cell contained a tiny but
complete replica of the mature plant or animal that had
only to enlarge its size. (The question of where those microscopic effigies came from caused natural philosophers considerable trouble.) The rise of materialist philosophy in the
seventeenth century brushed Aristotle's spirits aside, and
the invention of the microscope put the miniature effigy
theory to rest. Which left developmental biologists dangling in the wind. When I was a schoolkid, they were still
doing a lot of hand-waving about genes and fissioning cells,
but they didn't know much more about morphogenesis
than did Aristotle. The discovery of the structure of DNA
by James Watson and Francis Crick in the 1950s made it
clear that this beautiful molecule was the basis for genetics
and reproduction, but huge mysteries remain about how
genes are expressed in space and time in such a way as to
lead to the orderly development of an organism.

One day in the late 1950s I was eating a brown-bag
lunch with a friend in the botanical garden of the University of California at Los Angeles. We were surrounded by a
wonderful profusion of plants of every size and shape —
trees, shrubs, vines, cacti, flowering plants. My friend, a
physicist, took it all in and said, "Mathematics." "What?"
I mumbled. "The way things grow," he replied. "It's all
mathematics. I don't know how, but it's gotta be mathematics." My face betrayed my skepticism. He continued: "The
DNA thing. A sequence of four chemical units arranged

along the double helix. It's a kind of mathematical code. I know it seems impossible, but I'm sure that someday we'll be able to write a mathematical algorithm to describe the development of a pomegranate or a vine." It turns out that my friend was amazingly prescient. But at the time I wasn't convinced. I was too much the poet then, too much agog at the sheer lusciousness of life to allow my friend to reduce the botanical garden to mere numbers. A few years later I read D'Arcy Thompson's *On Growth and Form*. The 1917 classic had just been reissued in an abridged paperback by Cambridge University Press. Thompson, apparently, agreed with my friend. His book offered a huge compendium of mathematical patterns observed in the structure and growth patterns of plants and animals. "Mathematics, it's all mathematics," Thompson seemed to say.

OK, but how does it happen? How can a single cell unfold a lady's slipper—or a human being? What magic draws the rabbit from the microscopic hat? Thompson and my friend were both keenly aware of the mathematical architecture of life, but neither of them had a clue how it happens. Even today the answer is still uncertain, but studies in computer modeling of plant development make the "Mathematics, it's all mathematics" theory seem less far-fetched. Using purpose-made programming languages, computer scientists can cause colorful gardens of virtual flowers to flourish on monitor screens. In the earliest studies, these artificial plants were not much more realistic than the stick figures drawn by children, but they grew, branched, and blossomed in response to their digital environment. They even evolved. In recent years, virtual plants generated by computer algorithms have become uncannily realistic, almost indistinguishable from photographs of real plants. Forests of pines with needles and cones. Fields of sunflowers. Rose gardens. Lily ponds. The digital plants grow, replicate, respond to external influences, mutate, evolve—all according to mathematical programs. Call it, if you will, virtual botany.

Granted, the virtual gardens we see on computer monitors are at present no more than arbitrary models of real plants, but they will certainly lead to fresh insights into the riddle of morphogenesis. The plants we watch growing and developing on screen are defined by strings of symbols— programs—that are far less complex than the information contained in a single cell's complement of DNA. At the very least, the algorithms of the virtual botanists make it clear that the morphogenesis of plants and animals is something less than miraculous. The lady's slipper, the bluebird, the beauty and splendor of a newborn human infant: these are the flowerings of a mathematical music beating in the root of life.

 Last Quarter Moon

Vital dust. That's what Nobel Prize-winning biologist Christian de Duve titles his popular book on the origin and evolution of life. He means several things by the term: first, that life begins and perhaps flourishes throughout the universe as microscopically small organisms; second, that life

is chemical; third, that the original stuff of the universe—
the primeval dust—bore within it the potentiality, even the
certainty, of achieving animation. His title also reminds us
that we live in a sea of animated dust—invisible spores
swimming on the wind. We breathe these seeds of life in
and out with every breath. Rusts. Smuts. Molds. Mildews.
Mosses. Mushrooms. Ferns. Given the quantity and variety of airborne reproductive germs, it might seem likely
that our lungs would become gardens of foreign organisms—the invasion of the body snatchers. But that's not
quite the way life works. Most airborne spores must alight
in a highly specific environment if they are to bear fruit.

Consider cedar-apple rust.

For more than thirty years I have walked the same path
back and forth to work through woods and meadows. Most
of what I see is familiar. The same plants return year after
year to the same places. The same birds nest in the same
trees. The same insects take wing in the same climates and
seasons. Still, it's the rare week that my walk doesn't offer a
surprise, something I haven't seen before. A coyote. A kingfisher. A wild columbine. A stinkhorn mushroom. Thirty
years is not nearly enough time to exhaust the astonishing
diversity of life, even in our tame backyards.

A few weeks ago, on a wet May morning, a spot of
bright orange caught my eye in a cedar tree across the
meadow. At first I thought I was seeing an oriole—then
two, then three. I brought out my binoculars and the tree
exploded with bulbs of orange, as if it had been decorated
for Christmas. Close inspection revealed dozens of reddish-
brown fleshy growths, round or liver-shaped, attached to

leaves. Each of these growths sprouted a mass of gelatinous orange tentacles, like some horrid fungal colony of the forest floor, or a sea anemone. Some of these masses of tentacles were as large as grapefruits. I had never seen anything remotely like them—part insect gall, part mushroom—almost extraterrestrial in the way they seemed to have taken over the cedars. A little research provided an identification. The tentacled spheres were the fruiting bodies of cedar-apple rust, caused by the fungus *Gymnosporangium juniperi-virginianae.*

How did this apparition come to be? Start in the springtime on a nearby apple tree. Small yellow dots develop on the underside of the leaf shortly after the tree comes into bloom. The yellow spots gradually enlarge and become orange. Then black spots appear on the upper leaf surface. In late summer, small tubes grow on the lower leaf surface near the orange spots, and brown spots may develop on the fruit. The orange spots produce spores that are distributed by the wind. If they fall upon a cedar tree, they germinate and put out tubes that penetrate the tiny leaves. By some chemical magic, these tubes cause the growth of fleshy, reddish-brown galls, called cedar apples. The development of the galls and the maturing of the fungus within them require nearly two years from the time of infection. Then, during wet weather in May, the galls put out long slimy orange tentacles. These are composed of a different sort of spores that make their way by wind back to an apple tree. The cedar tree and the apple tree are necessary alternate hosts to the fungal parasite.

Generally, only apple growers are concerned about

these details of the cedar-apple rust's life cycle. But the story is an extraordinary parable of the interwoven texture of life: all those spores, at different stages of the fungus's life cycle, wafting back and forth at the mercy of the breezes, utterly dependent upon making an appropriate landing on a specific plant. And what I have provided here is only a rough sketch of the story, leaving out the wonderful chemical details. A complete molecule-by-molecule description of the life cycle of cedar-apple rust would fill a book, if it were known at all. For Christian de Duve, the author of *Vital Dust,* the life cycle of the *Gymnosporangium juniperi-virginianae* fungus would be just one more example of a life force that is deeply embedded in the creation, a "cosmic imperative," he calls it. He writes: "The history of life on Earth allows less leeway to contingency and unpredictability than current fashion [in science] claims." There is accident in the details, he believes, but inevitability in the grand thrust toward chemical complexity.

I think Christian de Duve is right. Life is too diverse, resilient, and pervasive not to have been built in from the beginning, at least in broad outline. You'd have to see a cedar tree full of orange-tentacled galls to dream that such a thing, almost otherworldly in its dissimilarity to anything else in our local environment, could exist. After I had done my research, I returned to the meadow—and stood there shaking my head with awestruck astonishment. Vital dust. Vital dust, indeed!

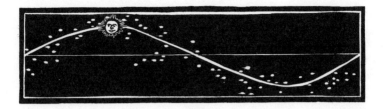

Summer Solstice

New Moon

Childhood has two seasons: anticipation and summer. Or so it seems in the mirror of memory. And it is memory, after all, that decides what matters in the long run. Autumns, winters, and springs of childhood blend in a fading reminiscence of galoshes, lunch boxes, slicked-back hair, school buses, multiplication tables, asphalt playgrounds, chalk dust, penmanship drills, calendars, and clocks — of staring listlessly out of classroom windows and counting the weeks, days, and minutes until the last bell of the last school day announces deliverance into nature. As the school year ends, the sun has reached its highest place in the sky. It is the solstice, which means literally "sun stands." Time stops and the calendar becomes an irrelevancy. Shoes are discarded. Shorts replace trousers and pleated skirts. Brushes and combs fall into disuse as hair goes tousled and free. Summer! Stickball in the meadow. Messing about in drainage ditches. Playing tag on twilit lawns as the brilliant

109

stars of summer—Arcturus, Vega, Deneb, Altair—come on like street lamps, guiding us to sleep made fitful by the day's unfinished projects, tomorrow's promises. The Earth's northern pole tips toward the sun, pushing back the bedtime hour, advancing the hour of dawn. Best of all were those nights we slept under the stars. The sounds of crickets, cicadas, and nocturnal birds—the amorous woodcock and the insomniac mockingbird—lulled us into slumber. Sometimes we woke in the still-warm night to find the Milky Way flowing from horizon to horizon like a cool stream—yawning, silent infinities observed from tangled blankets at the midnight hour, exhilarating and a little frightening.

My personal memories of the summer solstice are inevitably influenced by that most magical of chapters in Kenneth Grahame's *The Wind in the Willows,* "The Piper at the Gates of Dawn." *Midsummer eve.* The sun has set. Mole and Rat push off in their boat to look for Portly, the infant otter, who has gone missing from his home. They row upstream in moonlight. The night is full of animal noises— song and chatter and rustling. Meadowsweet, rose and purple loosestrife fringe the river's banks, perfuming the still air. Mole and Rat pass the night in dreamy, silent reverie, rowing and drifting on the purling stream, searching for the lost otter. Near dawn they hear a magical sound, a melody on pipes, that draws them to an island hemmed with willow, birch, and alder, cradled in a weir. "Here, in this holy place, here if anywhere, surely we shall find Him," whispers Rat, and it is not only Portly that he means. In a clearing on the island Mole and Rat find themselves in an august Presence — goat-hoofed, pipe-playing, great god Pan. And nestled between Pan's hooves, the sleeping infant otter. As the sun's first rays lance across the water meadow, the Vision vanishes and the air is full of caroling birds greeting the dawn. With the sun comes forgetfulness. Was the Vision real? Or was it a dream? Mole and Rat know that something exciting and rather terrible has happened, yet, it seems, nothing particular has happened. As they row home with the rescued otter, the whispering reeds bid them to forget.

How long ago and far away now seem those summer nights of childhood. What was it we found under the burning stars? Something was there, certainly, something exciting and rather terrible, a Presence if you will, a power in nature that manifests itself in the way things flow, in the way things hold together — sun, moon, stars, creatures, plants — a Presence that children everywhere are particularly disposed to perceive, especially children who have been raised on pagan tales and the pipes of Pan. Most of my adult life, I think, has been spent trying to remember what it was that I experienced on those solstitial nights long ago. Most of my adult life has been a struggle to become a child again in nature's presence, to perceive nature's flow and wholeness and my place in it with a child's purity of sight, to see and hear again the twinkling, shining, chattering, fluttering, rustling fullness of overbrimming creation, to resist with all my might the words whispered by the wind in the reeds: *You shall look on my power at the helping hour, but then you shall forget.*

First Quarter Moon

Firefly evenings long ago in Tennessee. Lingering twilight, dark pines, crickets singing, stars just coming into the sky. We were young, barefooted, our skinny legs festooned with the scabs of a hundred mosquito bites. Up and down the long, sloping lawn we ran, catching "lightnin' bugs" in our cupped hands. We squeezed them gently between our fingers to set their phosphorescent fires alight, or dumped them by the dozens into jam jars to make "lanterns." Cicadas, too! We caught them as they emerged from their nymphal skins, which they left attached to the trunks of trees, perfect hollow replicas of themselves, legs and all. It was fun to place these crisp brown shadow-bugs on Mom's sleeve to give her a start; she always pretended fright. Sometimes we tied Mom's sewing thread to the leg of a live cicada and set it buzzing at the end of a tether like a self-powered kite.

When we had outgrown these idle insect pleasures we took up serious collecting, especially butterflies and moths. Cardboard from Dad's freshly laundered shirts served as setting boards. Mounting pins came from Mom's sewing basket. Pickle jars were our killing bottles, filled with wads of cotton soaked in whatever kitchen fluid we thought would do the job—vinegar, cleaning fluid, even whiskey if we could snitch it. The deaths were never quick. At the end of summer we might have a dozen shirt boards decorated with insects, neatly labeled and classified—"Big Butterflies," "Little Butterflies," "Moths"—our first excursion into science. There weren't any school science fairs in those days, at least not where I lived. No teachers or parents badgered us to produce some suitably impressive project that might win a prize. We collected, killed, and pinned our bugs to boards because it was fun: the pure pleasure of running barefoot through a meadow with Mom's hairnet attached to a circle of coat-hanger wire in pursuit of a pair of flitting cabbage whites, or feeling a fat brown moth flail its powdery wings against the prison of our cupped hands.

The literature of amateur butterfly collecting is full of such disinterested summer pleasures. Virginia Woolf often returns in her writings to the childhood pursuits of butterflies and moths. She took her collecting seriously and, with her siblings Vanessa and Thoby, imposed upon her parents for proper apparatus: nets, collecting boxes, setting boards, killing bottles, cabinets, and appropriate works of reference. We, of course, had none of those. Our display cabinet was an orange crate, and our only reference source was my father's half-baked repertoire of entomologic lore. Here is how Woolf's biographer Quentin Bell describes the children's collecting activities: "As blood sports go, the killing of lepidoptera has a good deal to recommend it: it can offend only the most squeamish of humanitarians; it involves all the passion and skill of the naturalist, the charm of summer excursions and sudden exhilarating pursuits, the satisfaction of filling gaps in the collection, the careful study of text books, and, above all, the mysterious pleasure of staying up late, and walking softly through the night to where a rag, soaked in rum and treacle, has attracted dozens of slugs, crawly-bobs and, perhaps, some great lamp-eyed, tipsy, extravagantly gaudy moth." There is much in this voluptuous passage that evokes the pleasures of my own childhood, with the exception of the rum and treacle, those peculiarly British items, neither of which were part of our American experience. But once, just once, we found against the wall of the house a fabulously green luna moth, big, swallow-tailed, hugely gaudy. We quailed to catch it, partly out of fear, partly from awe; it seemed a sacrilege to subject such a magnificent creature to the indignity of our pickle-jar killing chamber.

The novelist Vladimir Nabokov is another writer who returns often to the butterfly collecting of his youth (as an adult he became an accomplished lepidopterist). From the age of seven, butterflies became his passion, provoked, in the first instance, by a rare and splendidly colored swallow-tail he found sitting on a honeysuckle bush in the garden of his home in Russia. He used ether as his killing agent, and later, as an adult undergoing an appendectomy, the smell of the chemical evoked a dream of a boy in a sailor suit killing and mounting an emperor moth: "It was all there, brilliantly reproduced in my dream, while my own vitals were being exposed: the soaking, ice-cold absorbent cotton pressed to the insect's lemurian head; the subsiding spasms of its body; the satisfying crackle produced by the pin penetrating the hard crust of its thorax; the careful insertion of the point of the pin in the cork-bottomed groove of the spreading board; the symmetrical adjustment of the thick, strong-veined wings under neatly affixed strips of semi-transparent paper."

The amateur entomologist, and particularly the untutored youthful collector, has a certain advantage over the professional, as the great Harvard entomologist William Morton Wheeler observed in one of his essays. Wheeler lamented that professionals tend to become obsessed by technical problems and are less open to the emotional and aesthetic joys of their discipline. He feared that one day he would find himself in the world beyond the Styx with other professional biologists, condemned forever to resolving minute questions of nomenclature and classification, while amateur entomologists roamed among "the fragrant asphodels of the Elysian meadows, netting gorgeous, ghostly butterflies until the end of time." We can hope that Wheeler has found an Elysian meadow and the comradeship there of Woolf and Nabokov. As for myself, I have become too enamored of life to any longer find pleasure in collecting. What remains of those childhood excursions with net and killing bottle are memories of the insect-filled joys of summer (an elegant viceroy or extravagantly colored swallowtail might be the prize of a summer's collecting, with an entire shirt board to itself, resplendent in the orange crate among cardboards crammed with dozens of coppers, fritillaries, and blues), and a lingering respect for the profligacy of a world that can contrive such a diversity of animate beauty.

 Full Moon — Hay Moon

I was raised a Roman Catholic, and something of that faith clings to me like a sweet odor that won't wash away. A sense of ritual. A sense of mystery. A sense of the sacred and the sacramental. A profound attraction to the symbolic possibilities of earth, air, fire, and water. I have drifted away from the the profession of the Creed, yet I retain an indelible affinity for the tradition of creation mysticism that has been strong in the Roman faith. That tradition rests comfortably with the other faith of my childhood—a kid's playful grounding in the sacraments of natural history. Little did I know, as I dumped fireflies into jam jars or squeezed their flashlight bodies, that I was absorbing a practical grace that would stand me in good stead long after the rituals of First Communion and Confirmation were forgotten.

A few years ago, I attended a gathering of nature writers on Martha's Vineyard in Massachusetts. On the first morning, we took time to introduce ourselves and say how we came to be interested in the natural world. I was struck by how often it was the experience of a drainage ditch that turned us toward nature. Few of us grew up in wild places. We were mostly children of the suburbs. More often than not it was while mucking about in a drainage ditch that we discovered what would become the passion of our lives. A drainage ditch can be a surprisingly rich habitat, especially compared with the green monotony of suburban lawns. Of course, as kids, we were not doing anything that could remotely be called natural history. We seldom knew the names of the plants and animals we observed, much less anything of their biology. The word *ecology* wasn't in our vocabulary, or even in our parents' vocabulary. But there were plenty of ditchy wonders to ignite a child's mind, to turn a child on forever to the richness of the natural world. Show me the kid who, having discovered the inconspicuous downward-pointing barbs on the stems of *Polygonum arifolium,* doesn't invite a friend to pull the plant from the ground; not for nothing is it called "tearthumb." Or the seed pods of jewelweed, a.k.a. touch-me-not; ask a companion to pinch a ripe seed pod and—*POW*—it explodes between her fingers. Cattails, perhaps the most unflowerlike flower in the ditch, were terrific clubs for ditchside frays, especially when ripe with fuzz.

Best of all were goldenrod galls. There is a tiny fly, *Eurosta solidaginis,* of the fruit fly family, that lays her eggs on fresh goldenrod stems in early summer. An egg hatches and the larva burrows into the stem, where it excavates a tiny cavity and feeds upon the tissue of the plant. By some sort of chemical sabotage, the insect causes the goldenrod to grow a fat round ball of tumorous tissue around its cavity. Inside this cozy globe the larva winters. In spring, the larva becomes active and chews a tunnel out to—but not through—the skin of the gall. Then it retreats to the center and pupates, rearranging its molecules to become an adult fly. The fly crawls down the tunnel, pops the skin, and emerges to mate, lay eggs, and start the cycle again. We looked for goldenrod galls in last year's plants at the side of the ditch. We broke the stems off at the base of the plant, and then again just above the gall. With these drumstick weapons we went about rapping each other over the head. We called them knockers. Sometimes two galls will form on a single goldenrod stem: a double knocker. A triple knocker was a prized rarity. Once I found a quadruple knocker that made me the envy of the neighborhood. None of us knew that inside each knocker was one or more goldenrod gallfly larva being shaken from its winter repose by the thumping violence of our battles.

There were other ways we used plants for mischief. Mature puffball mushrooms made marvelous smoke bombs to hurl at opponents. A popgun of sorts could be contrived by wrapping the bottom of the stem of a plantain around the top of the stem just at the base of the flower head and pulling sharply. We waged warfare with buckets of acorns, using the lids of steel trash cans for shields. We reveled bravely in the *ping-ping* of well-directed missiles hitting the metal just a few inches in front of our noses. We devised all sorts of devious stratagems for getting dandelion seed puffs into someone's mouth; extracting those little parachutes was devilishly difficult. Then, after our revels, we retired to the ditch bank to smoke "rabbit tobacco," the dried leaves of a plant called sweet everlasting that made us slightly ill but supplied a hint of illicit sophistication. Mother Nature was not stingy with playthings, particularly weapons, but somehow we survived our boyish propensity for knocking and smoke-bombing and acorn-hurling and grew up to be reasonably responsible citizens. What some of us took from the galls and the puffballs and the acorns and the sweet everlasting was a lifelong interest in the natural environment. While rapping each other over the head, we had the opportunity of falling in love with the natural world—so deeply, so knocked-out irreversibly, that the attraction lasted a lifetime.

The drainage ditch was a seasonal zodiac of frogs,

newts, salamanders, mudpuppies, crayfish, turtles, and snakes, fun to catch, keep, or simply use to scare the pants off timid comrades or any girl who dared to intrude upon our manly pleasures. Ditch water, in dribble or in flood, is the stuff of creaturedom, the great animator that turns cracked suburban mud into Darwin's tangled bank. Loose-strifes soak their feet in it. Knotweeds slurp it up. Water striders stride and whirligigs whirl on its slovenly surface. Even a trickle is an invitation to play: dams, canals, bridges, boats. Squishing barefoot in the mud among the cattails, shattering the great rose-window webs of argiope spiders, we were struck unconsciously and unalterably with the prodigiousness of life: a burry, buggy, algae-slicked intro-duction to nature's inexhaustible capacity to surprise. "The flowering of ditches" is Thoreau's delicious phrase. And looking back, I can see now that the experience was more than play: it was a kind of religious training, an intimate in-troduction to the Creator through his work, the creation. After all, didn't Jesus meet John the Baptist standing in a ditch, saying, "Prepare ye the way of the Lord."

My own childhood drainage ditch was in fields behind my house in Chattanooga, Tennessee, dug by whatever farmer owned the land to channel away the occasional flood. We played "army" on the banks, building roads and fortifications for our tin soldiers, Allies and Axis. We sent battalions floating on wood-chip barges to make amphibi-ous landings on the opposite shore. There was always the possibility that the snake seen slithering among the weeds might be the dreaded cottonmouth, which of course we never actually encountered, and which probably didn't even exist within a hundred miles of our ditch, but which, like the Loch Ness monster, imbued our murky waters with a captivating element of danger, a Leviathan of biblical proportions to inhabit the shallow deep. When play was finished we spent long hours sprawled on two-by-eight planks across the stream, lazily watching whatever gifts the muddy flow brought our way, a purling cornucopia of animals and plants. The fields of my childhood have now been built over with houses, but when last I was home the ditch was still there, sometimes channeled through concrete culverts, sometimes diverted to accommodate new roads, but still, one hopes, providing a provident hunting ground for a new generation of kids. When we have paved over all of the woods and fields, when chemically addicted lawns stretch in unbroken boredom from sea to sea, there will still be drainage ditches. Down at the back of the subdivision, at the side of the road, behind the mall. Places for kids to discover the tangled webs we have broken, nature's tattered but still living flesh, the final habitat.

 Last Quarter Moon

A mosquito bite, scratched into a scab, picked into a wound is a child's badge of a successful summer. Bare legs pocked with crusty sores are the willingly paid price of staying up late, having fun. Mosquitoes are to summer as stars are to the heavens—constant, uncountable, inextinguishable.

Children pay them little mind; adults are driven to distraction by the whispered drone of a mosquito near the ear at night. We have more in common with these insects than you might think. We share an ancestor in deep time, our kinship revealed by molecular biologists at the level of the genes. We share much of our basic molecular machinery. Certainly, we are chemically enough alike so that human blood protein is useful for the mosquito. We share the over-arching purpose of all living things—to survive long enough to reproduce. And our lives are bound inextricably together by the malaria parasite. In the United States and most developed parts of the world, we have more or less forgotten malaria. However, several million people world-wide suffer from this debilitating illness; more than one million die each year, mostly children. The cause of the disease is a microscopic creature called *Plasmodium*. Follow for a moment as I unravel *Plasmodium*'s remarkable life cycle.

The mosquito that bites us has only one thing on her mind: a blood meal. And it is definitely a she. Male mosquitoes have two things on their minds: sex and nectar. And only enough nectar to provide energy for sex. The male mosquito isn't interested in blood. It's the female that bites. She needs protein-rich blood to nourish her eggs. It need not be human blood, but by increasing our numbers at the expense of other species we have willy-nilly made ourselves the most readily available item on her menu. She may take more than one blood meal during her lifetime, which, as we shall see, can have unfortunate consequences for her second victim. If you are a female mosquito's first bite, don't worry. However, if she comes to you after biting someone who is infected with the malaria parasite, make sure you are slathered with repellent.

When a malarial mosquito of the genus *Anopheles* bites a human, she injects a bit of saliva, an anticoagulant, into the wound to keep the victim's blood flowing freely. In the saliva are thousands of tiny threadlike creatures called sporozoites. The sporozoites are carried by the bloodstream to the victim's liver, where they leave the blood and penetrate a liver cell. Inside, the sporozoite transforms itself into a sporelike form called a merozoite and replicates itself over and over, destroying the liver cell and building a cyst that is jam-packed with merozoites. After two weeks, the cyst bursts and spews its contents into the bloodstream. Each merozoite attaches itself to a human red blood cell and enters it. The merozoite feeds on hemoglobin, growing bigger, until it shatters into bits, each of which becomes another merozoite. At last, the blood cell explodes its teeming contents back into the bloodstream. The process repeats itself over and over, while the human host goes through recurring bouts of fever.

But now an amazing thing happens. After several cycles of replication, some of the merozoites become sexual forms called gametocytes, male and female. These circulate in the bloodstream until the host is bitten by another *Anopheles* mosquito, seeking blood to nourish her eggs. The gametocytes are sucked up by the mosquito along with their asexual merozoite companions. The blood-gorged *Anopheles* flies away from its human victim. Inside her stomach the asexual merozoites die. Male gametocytes turn themselves into swarms of lashing, spermlike filaments that penetrate the female gametocytes and fertilize them. Each fertilized "egg" now transforms itself into a creepy-crawly thing that bores through the mosquito's stomach wall, where it attaches itself to the outside of the stomach and becomes a cyst. Within the cyst, the material of the "egg" reorganizes itself into thousands of threadlike forms, the sporozoites. The cyst bursts, the sporozoites make their way to the mosquito's salivary gland, and—and wait like bullets in a loaded gun for the mosquito to have her second blood meal. A new victim, a new life cycle for *Plasmodium*.

This is the condensed version of the story. I have left out, for example, the many ingenious tricks that *Plasmodium* employs to outwit the human immune system.

Humans are necessary to *Plasmodium*'s life cycle, as cafeterias for feeding and bowers for sexual reproduction. The *Anopheles* mosquito is necessary as a vehicle for transport and a place of sexual expression. For malaria to be endemic, all three members of this diabolic waltz must be present— human, mosquito, and parasite. It is often said that mosquitoes kill more humans than any other animal, but it is not the mosquito that kills. It is the parasites they carry, most especially the malaria pathogen, *Plasmodium*. With our clever brains and scientific skills we are not passive victims. We marshal our resources. We discover or invent drugs to attack the pathogen or mitigate the symptoms of the disease. We drain swamps where *Anopheles* lays her eggs. We spray with pesticides. And for a while, these strategies worked. Some parts of the world, the United States for example, have become malaria free (although, alas, not mosquito free). The incidence of malaria worldwide temporarily diminished, and for a while there was optimism that the malaria pathogen might be driven to extinction. But *Anopheles* and *Plasmodium* are not without resources of their own—particularly their quick reproductive cycles. Darwinian natural selection brushed them with its favoring wings. Within mere decades *Anopheles* evolved immunity against pesticides. *Plasmodium* evolved resistance to drugs. Evolution outran human ingenuity. After a period of decline, malaria is resurging. Today, malaria is the leading cause of death worldwide for children under five.

All of this is something to ponder during summer as mosquitoes buzz. The evolutionary river that flows out of Eden binds us together in a common fate—human, mosquito, malaria protozoa. Try as we might, there is no way we can extract ourselves from the stream. Each of us is doing everything we can to increase the odds of our own survival, and evolution favors the species with the quickest reproductive cycle. Which isn't us. *Slap!*

 New Moon

Remember the shmoo? The shmoo was invented by Al Capp in the comic strip "Li'l Abner": a wobbly, tenpin-with-legs sort of creature with the misfortune (or good fortune) of being almost totally consumable. Broiled shmoo tasted like steak; fried, like chicken. Shmoos gave eggs, butter, and Grade A milk. The shmoo's skin was a versatile fabric, the eyes made perfect buttons, and even the whiskers served as toothpicks. Most important, shmoos reproduced in prodigious numbers and delivered themselves willingly to human appetites. If you looked hungrily at a shmoo, it dropped dead of happiness. Shmoos were cute, shmoos were adorable. Shmoos were also irresistible blobs of protein. Their happy destiny was to be someone else's dinner.

Now, think about it another way. Humans reproduce with shmoolike abandon. Never in the history of the planet has a single species multiplied with so few constraints. There are at present nearly six billion of us, and our numbers are soaring. We level forests, fill bays, drain wetlands, and pave over prairies to provide living space for our burgeoning progeny. We have made ourselves the shmoos of the planet—irresistible foodstuffs. Zoologist Mark Ridley writes: "Just as we consume resources, so we are ourselves a resource to be consumed. So far, we merely happen to be extraordinarily underexploited. . . . There is no ecological opportunity on the earth to compare with the gigacaloric potential of human flesh." In other words, we are a bounteous meal waiting to happen.

But who will eat us? We are at the top of the food chain, more or less. The few man-eating predators on the planet can be held at bay with weapons; indeed, as our own numbers increase, sharks, lions, and tigers are pushed toward extinction. In developed parts of the world, biting insects are a mere nuisance, held in temporary check by a host of chemical pesticides. What about extraterrestrials? Might we become the grub of a more advanced galactic race? Maybe, but the possibility is too remote to bear worrying about. No, the real eaters who are waiting to consume us are closer to home, and poised to escalate their terrible assault. I speak, of course, of the vast invisible communities of viruses and bacteria. With every bite of food we eat, we convert more of the available planetary resources into human flesh. Increasingly, we must look like shmoos to the microbes: plump, available, irresistible. There is a huge Darwinian pressure on microbes to make their diet out of us. So far, they have made only limited evolutionary progress toward overwhelming our defenses, but the dynamic of evolution is on their side.

Not to worry, you say. We have managed to keep lions and tigers at bay, we can do the same for microbes. Haven't we invented antibiotics that will do the trick? In some parts of the world, at least, we have driven the malaria pathogen into retreat. Smallpox and plague are extinct, or virtually so. Surely, no microscopic organism can compete with human genius. Well, don't be too sure. The story is more complicated than that. For one thing, it wasn't human genius that invented antibiotics. Penicillin and its allies were evolved by fungi and molds as defenses against bacteria. Humans discovered antibiotics when a penicillin-making mold accidentally fell into a dish of bacteria in the laboratory of Alexander Fleming in 1928. In other words, our famous "miracle drugs" are products of millions of years of evolutionary trial and error. What humans have done is steal the drugs from molds and fungi and use them against our own bacterial enemies. Unfortunately, we have used these precious weapons without restraint, placing a strong selective pressure on bacteria to evolve resistance—and of

course they have done so. The effectiveness of our antibiotic arsenal is fading fast. The blame for this sorry state of
affairs can be shared by drug companies for greedily hawk-
ing each new antibiotic, by doctors for overprescribing the
drugs, and by patients for insisting upon frivolous prescrip-
tions. Score a big one for the microbes.

Microbes have dominated the planet for nearly four billion years; the rest of us are fairly recent arrivals. Some
would say that microbes still own the planet and merely tolerate the so-called higher animals and plants as long as it
suits their purpose. An adult human's body is home to about
100 trillion microbial organisms, ten times more alien creatures than the number of cells of the body itself! They are
everywhere: eyes, ears, teeth, gums, between the toes, in the
groin. They harbor by the millions in the prairies of the skin,
the woodlands of the scalp, the rain forests of the armpits. A
spelunking tour of the body would take us through the res-
piratory tract, the oral cavity, the gastrointestinal tract, and
the outer part of the urinary tract, each with its swarming
population of microorganisms. Consider, for example, *Escherichia coli,* bean-shaped inhabitant of the human intestine.
It is a pinch of protoplasm in a sack, with a single chromo-
some and a loop of DNA that, if you stretched it out, would
just encircle the dot on this letter *i* (by contrast, each cell in
the human body has twenty-three chromosomes, contain-
ing altogether about an arm's length of DNA). Nevertheless, *E. coli* moves. It feeds. It reproduces. It recognizes
and communicates with its own kind. In a primitive sense, it
can even remember. It gets from here to there by wriggling
its whiplike appendages—or screwing them, actually, like

propellers. It has, such as it is, a mind of its own. A million *E. coli* laid end to end would make a line only as long as my arm, but there are enough of them inside me to form a line that would stretch from Boston to San Francisco. A significant part of my body weight is not me at all, but my burgeoning population of *E. coli*. As houseguests go, they are not unwelcome. They produce certain useful vitamins. They sometimes devour other less benevolent microorganisms that might do me harm. Biologists call our relationship "commensal," which means literally "eating at the same table." We tolerate them. More to the point, perhaps, they tolerate us. For the moment, it suits their purpose.

We survive as part of a precarious balance with bacteria and viruses. The black death of the Middle Ages, the influenza epidemics of the early twentieth century, and the AIDS scourge of our own time are reminders of what can happen when the balance is upset. The old myth of our God-given dominion over the planet is not only wrong, it is downright dangerous. As the human population explosion increasingly turns the biomass of the planet into human flesh, the ancient balance between ourselves and the microbes is put at risk. The microbes have the advantage of short reproduction cycles, a million times faster than our own: in any race to evolve defenses against the enemy, we haven't a hope of competing. Bacteria can evolve resistance against antibiotics within months or years. Our own natural defense mechanisms against bacteria are the products of millions of years of evolution. We are sitting ducks, irresistible potential feasts, victims of our own success and lack of reproductive restraint.

First Quarter Moon

Anyone who has watched a dragonfly scout a summer pond has seen one of the wonders of evolution. A cross between a traffic chopper and an F-16. A flawless match of form and function. A flying machine optimized for snapping up insects on the wing. And for sex. But more of that in a moment.

Every now and then evolution throws up a creature so perfectly adapted to its way of life that improvement seems impossible. Such species are rewarded by longevity. They survive for eons with little change. They become what evolutionary biologists call living fossils. The dragonfly is a living fossil, one of the oldest orders in the animal kingdom. One famous dragonfly fossil from the Jurassic limestone of Germany is 200 million years old. Every wing vein is recorded with astonishing fidelity. The pattern matches in almost every detail the drawing of a dragonfly wing in my *Peterson Field Guide to Insects*. The fossil insect seems ready to take flight, released from a 200-million-year sleep to join its modern cousin. Dragonfly fossils have been found in rocks as old as the Carboniferous period of earth history, 300 million years ago. Some of these ancient fliers had wingspans exceeding two feet. Dinosaurs came and went, pterodactyls flourished and disappeared, thousands of species of mammals evolved and became extinct. Dragonflies go on and on; they are the Energizer bunnies of evolution. Sit by the summer pond and watch them. You might as well be in a time warp. Glance up and see *Triceratops* grazing nearby.

Or thundering *Tyrannosaurus rex*. Asteroids smash into Earth and the reptilian giants become extinct; the dragonfly survives.

Entomologists separate the order Odonata into dragonflies and the more delicate damselflies, but for most summer pond watchers, and in popular parlance, they are the same. Iridescent eyes, with tens of thousands of glittering facets. Shimmering blues and greens. Opal. Blood red. Ultramarine. No wonder dragonflies are talismans of summer, one of the few insects we welcome in this season of exposed skin. Graybacks, clubtails, darners, biddies, and skimmers. Their names evoke poetry. Popular names are even more evocative: water maidens, demoiselles, horse stingers, mosquito hawks, devil's darning needles, snake doctors. When I was a kid, I was told that dragonflies stitch up the eyes of sleeping children. They are also said to sew up the wounds of injured snakes.

But it is the flying skills of dragonflies that makes it possible to sit for hours beside the pond or stream, watching them move. Dragonflies may be the most elegant aviators on the planet. Forward, backward, straight up or down. Zip. Spin. Stop on a dime. Their center of gravity lies just below the base of the wings, with helicopter balance. Opposite wings are connected by strong flight muscles, and the two pairs of wings operate independently. A big dragonfly can reach an air speed of sixty miles per hour. Pure flying machine. The dragonfly's legs are made not for walking but for clutching a reed or twig when at rest. And for scooping up insects. The dragonfly uses its netted legs like a shopping cart. It has been known to gather up dozens of mosquitoes at a time.

I have a special place for watching aquatic insects, a plank bridge across a sluggish stream on conservation land. Lying prone, my face is only a foot from the surface of the water. There I observe water striders and whirligigs in late spring. Backswimmers in fall. And dragonflies in summer. The males take up territories near the banks of the stream. Perching on reeds or stones. Chasing off intruding males. Patrolling. It's a macho sort of thing. Establishing priority. The dominant male has the best chance to mate. But there's a bit of business that must be taken care of first. The male's genital opening is near the tip of his tail. The penis, however, is just behind the legs. So before he mates, the male dragonfly must transfer sperm from the tip of the tail to the penis up front. Then he grasps the female behind her head with the tip of his tail. She curls her abdomen around and under until she brings her genital organ—at the tip of her tail—to his penis. Now their bodies are engaged in a heart-shaped configuration, one of nature's more engagingly semiotic acts of copulation. Sometimes they stay in this valentine grasp for a perplexingly long time, perhaps to ensure fertilization, or maybe because they're too love-besotted to let go. Many dragonflies do not disengage even when they disentangle. They dart about in tandem, the male still grasping the female's neck while she lays her eggs. Every pond watcher has seen these linked pairs, as adept at doubled postcoital flight as when solitary.

Evolutionists tell us that silverfish are the most ancient

insects that survive more or less unchanged into the present. Cockroaches and dragonflies are almost as old. Of these living fossils only the dragonfly is an unmitigated boon to humans. It bears no human pathogens. It doesn't bite. It eats insects that do bite. An iridescent exterminator. A welcome companion of summer. A 300-million-year-old beauty on the wing.

Dingle

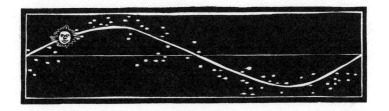

Lammas

◯ Full Moon — Green Corn Moon

I spend part of each year in a house on a hill in the west of Ireland. The place is a castle in the air. The view out of every window is atmospheric, ever changing, an operatic play of wind, water vapor, and light. We have no television; the drama of the air is entertainment enough. I have never visited any other place with so *much* weather. Hailstones the size of marbles thumping on the slates. Mists oozing through the mountain passes like molasses. Rainbows out the bedroom window in the mornings, out the living room window in the evenings. Stars glimpsed through masses of moonlit cloud. Soft days (as the Irish say) and days of raging gales. This is the Earth at its dynamic best, Gaia gauzed in furl and flurry. The movement of the crustal plates that transform the rocky surface of the Earth are too slow to be observed on the human scale. The currents that stir the oceans are mostly hidden by depth and opacity. But in the atmosphere Gaia flaunts her vivacity, allowing us enough transparency to observe great expanses of air, yet revealing her movements with signatures of cloud.

What is the air? Thoreau, in one of his more rhapsodic moments, called it "a foundry full of molds for casting bluebirds' warbles." His flamboyant metaphor is not far off the mark. The subtle warps and crevices of air, defined by temperature, pressure, and movement, can indeed give shape to sound, teasing a bluebird's call far out across a summer meadow, or slurring the vibrancy of the warble. Similarly, air gives shape to light, life, and spirit. "The air," said Thoreau, "is as deep as our natures."

Physically, the air is less deep than we are likely to suppose. Cover a bowling ball in a single layer of plastic kitchen wrap and you have a pretty good scale model of Earth and its atmosphere. Within that wisp-thin envelope are all of the phenomena of air: the tumbling clouds, the bluebird's call, the flights of kites and bumblebees, rainbows, hurricanes, pea-soup fogs, acrid smogs, scarlet sunsets, the flicker of fireflies, and the hoots of owls. The only problem with the kitchen-wrap model is that the real atmosphere has no well-defined upper boundary. The planet's gassy envelope yields with increasing tenuousness to the vacuum of space; in other words, it gets thinner and thinner until it isn't there anymore. Nevertheless, once we have ascended ten miles above Earth's surface—or about the thickness of the kitchen wrap compared to the bowling ball—most of the atmosphere is below us. The lower ten miles or so of the atmosphere is called the troposphere, from the Greek *tropos,* for "change" or "turn." This is where most of the action takes place. Within this thin shell of air, temperatures decrease with altitude, dropping as low as minus 80 degrees Fahrenheit near the top. These dramatic temperature variations, together with the rotation of the planet, set up the global movements of air that cause our weather.

Above the troposphere, in the stratosphere, ultraviolet radiation from the sun warms the air, causing the temperature to rise again to a relatively balmy 65 degrees. This is the realm of ozone, a form of oxygen that absorbs the sun's ultraviolet radiation, protecting life on the surface of the Earth from deadly short-wavelength light. Here, too, cosmic rays (high-energy particles from space) collide with air molecules and splatter into showers of less energetic—and less harmful—secondary particles. The stratosphere is mostly cloud free, and therefore virtually invisible from the surface, but it provides us with indispensable protection against dangers from space. Above the stratosphere, at altitudes of thirty to fifty miles, the temperature plummets again. This is where meteors burn up, heated by friction with rarefied air, creating those streaks of burning vapor we call "shooting stars" or "falling stars." Wisps of ice crystals in the upper mesosphere sometimes catch rays of sunlight after darkness has fallen on the surface, shining with a pale ethereal light—the so-called noctilucent ("night-shining") clouds. Another reversal of temperature occurs above fifty miles, in the thermosphere, where exceedingly thin air is heated by solar radiation to temperatures of thousands of degrees. Atoms are stripped of electrons by radiation, creating charged ions that effect long-distance electromagnetic communication, and sometimes make it possible for my spouse to pick up faraway stations on her shortwave radio. Here, too, energetic particles streaming from the sun collide with molecules of air, exciting them to luminescence and igniting spectacular auroral displays near the Earth's poles. The thermosphere extends to several hundred miles above the surface—about a quarter of an inch above the surface of the bowling ball—to the realm of low-orbiting satellites. This is the threshold of space, and for all practical purposes, the top of the atmosphere.

Every layer of the atmosphere contributes to our well-being; every layer enhances the visual beauty of the sky. Storms, rainbows, meteors, noctilucent clouds, auroras, satellites: we watch them all from our Irish castle in the air, a never-ending theater of spacy grandeur. What we can't observe from the Earth's surface is the kitchen-wrap *thinness* of the atmosphere. On the human scale, the atmosphere seems to reach to the stars, a vast and inviolable munificence of air. Photographs of Earth from space reveal a different picture. We see the planet on its own scale, suspended in the inky dark of space, skinned with cloud. How fragile the atmosphere appears in the space photographs, how wispy thin! Only the gentle tug of gravity holds it to the surface against the tendency of a gas to expand into a vacuum. The Earth acquired its skin of air at its fiery beginning. More than four billion years ago the planet was mostly molten, or almost so—a planet-encompassing volcano. From the seething surface bubbled up the gases that became the first atmosphere. The atmosphere was different then than now, probably much more like the present-day atmosphere of Venus and Mars, with large components of carbon dioxide and almost no oxygen. The present atmosphere is one-fifth oxygen and almost no carbon dioxide. The difference is due to liquid water and life. Carbon dioxide readily combines with water to form insoluble carbonates, which precipitate to the bottom of the sea and harden into the rocks we know as limestone and dolomite. Animals and plants in the sea take up carbonates to build their skeletons and shells; at death, these also fall to the sea bottom as part of rock-forming sediments. If you are looking for the carbon dioxide that was in the Earth's earliest atmosphere, you could do no better than to start with the limestone rocks of Ireland's Vale of Tralee. And what about the oxygen? Where did it come from? Most of the oxygen was contributed by life, as a by-product of photosynthesis. For a billion years, Earth's atmosphere has been in balance with animals, plants, sea, and rocks. The gases of the air are cycled and recycled through the rocky crust, oceans, atmosphere, and biosphere, in a kind of breath that resembles our own. It is a grand engine, or metabolism, depending on whether you prefer a mechanical or a biological metaphor. It is an ongoing process, delicately tuned, adjusting itself with the deliberate languor of evolution.

As I watch the voluminous heavings of air from the window of my Irish hillside house, it is difficult to imagine that any human activity might change the product of eons. But none of us should doubt the capacity of life to impose its nature upon the air; one need only compare Earth's atmosphere to that of Venus or Mars to see the transforming efficacy of life. What is new is technology, which amplifies the speed of change, outpacing the capacity of geologic process and biological evolution to adapt, disrupting a balance patiently contrived at Gaia's own unhurried pace. The Greek word *pneuma* can be translated as "wind," "breath," or "spirit." The atmosphere is all of that. It is *pneuma*. It is *tropos*. It is kitchen-wrap thin. It is a foundry of bluebirds' warbles. It is the medium of voice, song and music. It is the wind that even as I write blows sheets of rain against the windows of our house. It is the breath of life. And, as Thoreau said, it is as deep as our natures.

 ## Last Quarter Moon

It had rained in sheets for forty days and forty nights. At last, the downpour subsided and the level of the flood began to fall. The tip of Carrantuohill mountain, Ireland's highest, emerged like a tiny island in the sea, and Noah made for it. As he stepped ashore from the ark he met a rain-drenched Irishman, who greeted him: "A fine soft day, thanks be to God."

A fine soft day, indeed. Here in Kerry, it has misted, showered, or lashed down rain not forty days these past several months, but eighty. Nights, too. Fogging the windows. Spattering the roof. Streaming down the backs of our necks and legs to fill our rubber boots. Water sluices from the hills. The fields are carpets of squish. Carrantuohill mountain is outside my window, beyond Dingle Bay, but today I can't see it. The sky is saturated with moisture, a humidity of 110 percent, as heavy with water as a soaked sponge. Valentia Island is out there, too, hidden in the cloud, one of Ireland's official weather-reporting stations. The radio says visibility at Valentia is half a mile. I know, I know. In a typical Irish year some precipitation falls two days out of every three. Here in Kerry it can seem like three out of three. A place for ducks. Fish. What are the tourists doing here? What am *I* doing here?

Ah, the answer is obvious. The lushness, the green. The rank hedges of fuchsia, the banks of montbretia. The sky like an ever-changing watercolor painting, clouds piled like peat ricks, heaped in billows. Rainbows, morning and evening; sometimes I've seen five or six rainbows in a single day. The snugness of the pub with its glowing fire. The gorgeous everyday purity of the air, washed clean by rain and hung out to dry in a sparkling sun. Ireland would not be Ireland without the rain. With a bit more sunshine our Kerry beach would be barricaded with high-rise hotels, like the built-up coastlines of the Mediterranean and Florida. Instead, we have long, lonely stretches of sand swept into pristine dunes, litter-free beach grass, crystal-clear water lapping our feet—a beach where on a misty day we can still imagine the ghosts of Finn Mac Cool and the King of the World battling it out for a year and a day. No wonder the Italians and Spaniards and Floridians come here. Bless the rain. Bless whatever geographical quirk brings the drenchings to our shore.

It's all that warm water out there in the North Atlantic. The prevailing wind moves across the ocean from the west, soaking up moisture like a paper towel moving across a wet kitchen counter, to wring itself out on Ireland's west coast.

The warmer the ocean water, the more readily evaporation occurs and the wetter the wind. The North Atlantic Ocean is anomalously warm for its latitude. Why? The Gulf Stream. Or at least that's what we're told. We read it in books, newspapers, tourist brochures. The Gulf Stream laps Ireland's shore, bringing scents of the south, tropical breezes, palm trees, fuchsia. Mexican heat pumped northward on a river in the sea to give Ireland a mild, wet climate. That's what they say. But it's not so simple. True, the rivers in the sea are there. The South Equatorial Current flows across the top of South America into the Caribbean Sea. Four and a half million years ago it passed into the Pacific between North and South America, which were not yet connected. Then volcanic activity heaved up the isthmus at Panama. The tropical current was deflected northward into the Gulf of Mexico. There it is warmed further like water in a pan, finally escaping between Florida and Cuba to feed the Gulf Stream, an arrow of balmy heat aimed at Ireland. It's not quite clear what happens to all this liquid warmth. Somewhere near the Grand Banks of Newfoundland the boundaries of the stream get messy. The river in the sea dissolves into eddies of curling water. What's left of the Gulf Stream collides with the cold Labrador Current coming down from the north, then peels off southward to feed the current called the Azores Anticyclone. Some part of the tropical waters may join the North Atlantic Drift that actually reaches Ireland, stoking with its warmth the evaporation that douses Kerry.

But wait. Geochemist Wally Broecker of the Lamont-

Doherty Geological Observatory has another idea. Broecker has proposed a globe-spanning oceanic conveyor belt with its northern terminus in the North Atlantic. Cold winds from Canada blow across the water near Iceland, cooling it. The cold, dense water sinks, and flows as a deep bottom current southward around the Cape of Good Hope into the Indian and Pacific Oceans. There it rises, warms, and as a shallower current returns to the Atlantic and flows northward. Near Iceland, this warm water from tropical seas somehow makes it way to the surface and has its heat stolen away by Canadian winds — the genial, moisture-drenched westerlies that keep Ireland warm and wet. So, if Broecker is right, the source of the water hanging in the air outside my window is palm-fringed oceans on the other side of the world!

But who knows? Maybe some of the moisture in our westerly winds is picked up way back there near New-foundland, where the Gulf Stream is well and truly impli-cated. Maybe both oceanic circulations — the surface and the deep — are partly involved. All that we know for sure is that Ireland's winds come off a warm ocean, and therefore the climate here in Kerry, at latitude 52 degrees, is milder in winter and more equable all year round than at Boston, at latitude 42 degrees. That's why I choose to live here for a big part of the year, instead of Boston. That's why the tourists come in droves. But the price we pay for our mod-erate climate, green fields, fuchsia-choked lanes, wild wet hills, pristine beaches, and dazzling rainbows is nearly in-cessant precipitation. Fine soft days, thanks be to God. Weeks. Months. Years.

New Moon

It was the summer of the jellyfish. On some retreating tides, the beach was jammed with jellies. A walk at water's edge required constant attention to what was underfoot; few experiences are more unpleasant than stepping barefoot into a quivering cushion of jellyfish jelly. This year, the blobs of tentacled goo have been especially abundant on Irish coasts all summer long. On our beach the jellyfish are mostly of the species *Aurelia*, the common moon-jelly, the size of a dinner plate when flattened on the sand, with four elegant purple rings near the top of its transparent bell. The rings are the animal's sex organs. There's not much else to see. The fringe of stinging tentacles (not dangerous in *Aurelia*) and the dangling mouth-arms under the bell are mostly hidden once the jellyfish is stranded on the sand. From the kids at the water's edge comes a constant litany of "Yuck!" "Gross!" "Disgusting!" Poor kids. Poor jellyfish. Lemmings, according to a discredited myth, throw themselves of their own volition into the sea, and sometimes whales will beach themselves singly or en masse for reasons known only to whales. But jellyfish don't choose to inflict themselves on summer bathers. They travel at the whim of sea and weather, drifting where the currents take them, and if some combination of gyres and breezes dumps a thousand of them onto the sand where we want to swim, well, that's hardly the fault of the jellyfish.

Aurelia's lifestyle is altogether curious. Sometimes in late summer the adult jellyfish release eggs and sperm into the water. The free-swimming larvae resulting from fertilization attach themselves to rocks or seaweed on the seafloor and transform themselves into tiny plantlike polyps, each polyp shaped like a stack of inverted saucers. Thus anchored and secure, they pass the winter. In spring, the saucers bud off tiny jellyfish, which grow into big jellyfish, which — if winds and tides are perverse — find themselves high and dry and squashed by human feet. Jellyfish stranded on the sand don't have much of a future, even if they are spared the foot. They quickly die and evaporate. Their bodies are 99 percent water; they have fewer non-aqueous ingredients than weak lemonade. A mousse or a meringue is a Rock of Gibraltar compared to a jellyfish.

But mousses and meringues are not alive, and life is what it is all about. For all their simplicity, jellyfish are amazingly efficient at making other jellyfish. Their mix of water and jelly may be 99-to-1, but it appears to be an ideal recipe for survival. In the 1950s, geologist Martin Glaessner discovered rocks in the Ediacara Hills of southern Australia that contain fossils of the first multicelled organisms to flourish on this planet, a diverse community of soft-bodied creatures that was somehow buried in fine sand and preserved as delicate impressions in sandstone. The rocks are nearly 700 million years old. And who was there at the very beginning of multicelled life? You guessed it — the jellyfish. Armored trilobites, thunder-footed dinosaurs, and saber-toothed tigers have come and gone; the watery jellyfish have endured. They have outlasted animals with more bulk and more brains. Their strategy for survival has been spectacularly successful: keep it simple, go with the flow. In

jellyfish we see life reduced to its essentials. Under those
pretty purple reproductive rings are a mouth and four dangling arms with nothing to do except stuff the mouth. Eat
and drift, drift and eat; it's the original hobo existence. And
if you live in the sea, transparency is more or less equivalent
to invisibility—another survival secret of the hobo.

Jellyfish are not entirely without self-propulsion. In
quiet tide pools they manage to push themselves this way
and that by rhythmically contracting muscles (such as they
are) on the lower rim of the bell, but how they decide where
they are going is a mystery. They have eyes of a sort at the
base of their tentacles, and other rudimentary sensory organs, but it's hard to imagine that an inverted bowl of transparent slime can have much of an IQ. When great numbers
of them wash up on the beach, it is not intellect or will that
put them there, but quirks of circulation in the great global
engine of sea and air. And where did our hordes of *Aurelia*
come from? Probably rounded up cowboy-style by circu-
lating currents in Irish coastal waters and flung onto our
shore by a southwest wind. The fluke of their appearance in
such multitudes is part of that vast system of flukes we call
the weather. If meteorologists can't reliably predict the
weather two days from now (and around here they can't),
it's because the agitations of water and wind are so damn-
ably complicated.

The agitations of weather don't agitate the jellyfish.
They go wherever the currents and tempests take them.
Theirs may not be the most independent sort of existence
(and for the kids on the beach it can be positively yucky),

but it has served jellyfish well for 700 million years. In the great Darwinian struggle to survive, going with the flow has much to recommend it.

 First Quarter Moon

A dozen years ago at the end of a spell of fine summer weather we could look out from our house in the west of Ireland and count a thousand haystacks. Field after field of haystacks, as far as the eye could see. This summer, for the first time, there is not a haystack to be seen. The haystacks have been swept away by high-tech agriculture with disorienting speed.

I used to spend a few days each summer helping neighbors cut the grass with scythes, then, after the grass had dried on the ground, pitch it into stacks, and later still, carry it to the hay shed. It was hard, satisfying work on a sunny day, with an occasional cup of tea taken in the shade of a hedgerow and a tumbler of whiskey at day's end. My neighbors kept a wary eye on the weather; if the grass didn't dry on the ground and in the stack, it would rot in the shed and there would be nothing to sustain the animals through the winter. All of that is gone now: the scythes, the pitchforks, the aching muscles soothed by tea and whiskey. Instead, grass is cut for silage, stored green under airtight conditions. A popular technology uses a single combine to mow the grass, wrap it in opaque plastic, and pop the bundles out the back of the machine. Haystacks have been replaced in the fields by what look like giant black beach balls.

Nothing unusual about any of this; the haystack vanished a long time ago in most developed parts of the world. What is different about western Ireland (and other fringe areas of Europe) is how recent and swift the change has been. The transformation of the landscape happened even as we watched from our house on the hill. Ireland has been justly famous for its many tiny green fields separated by hedgerows. Now the hedgerows are rooted out by giant machines so that the silage makers can operate their giant machines more efficiently. There is no longer any need to rotate crops and animals among many small fields; farmers rely on artificial fertilizers to maintain the fertility of the land. Gone, too, are the oat sheaves stacked in shocks and fields of potatoes and turnips. One crop—grass for cattle—is enough to satisfy the farmer's need; vegetables for the table are bought at the supermarket. Productivity has soared. The result of these changes is money in the pocket, new homes and automobiles, multichannel satellite television, holidays at Disney World—in short, all of the standard material trappings of homogenized Euro-American consumer culture. These changes have also caused increased rural unemployment, the dispersal of families, diminution of wildlife, pollution of groundwater and streams by fertilizers, and contamination of the food chain by pesticides. Our neighbors have mixed feelings about the transformation of their traditional culture. They know something valuable has been lost, but such is the lavishness of technology's material gifts that they are unwill-

ing to hold on to the old ways. And who can blame them?
Certainly not me.

We came to Ireland many years ago to seek, for a few
months each year, a life that was less beholden to machines,
closer to nature, with less consumerism. We built a cottage
on a hill by the sea. No electricity. No washer, no dryer, no
telephone, no television, no central heating. We furnished
the house with handsaw, hammer, plane, needle, and
thread. Local craftspersons supplied crockery, rugs, deco-
rations. Travel was by bicycle or shank's mare. For a
decade our summers in Ireland were everything we hoped
they might be: annual retreats from frenzied servitude to
technology. Alas, technology nibbled away at the margins
of our simplicity until little is left of what we came to find.
Today, the house has electricity and a washing machine. A
gasoline-powered trimmer has replaced the scythe for keeping the yard groomed. Power tools do the work of handsaw
and plane. There is a sewing machine in the loft and an
automobile in the driveway. Electric heaters give occasional rest to the coal-burning stove. A telephone, computer modem, e-mail, and the Internet keep us in touch
with the world. In other words, flicks of the switch have replaced the trimming of wicks and the riddling of grates, and
all the good intentions in the world don't seem to stop the
intrusions of machines. What has happened to our "simple"
life in the west of Ireland is the same as what has happened
to the traditional agricultural community we see outside
our windows: machinery and economics of scale have ex-
erted their inexorable and compelling logic.

The haystacks are gone and with them a way of life lived

in harmony with nature. Now our neighbors must begin their struggle against consumerism, overdevelopment, litter, crime, the breakup of families, erosion of the Irish language, an end to a rich tradition of storytelling and music, despoliation of a spectacularly beautiful landscape, and — in this last unhurried paradise in the developed world — frenzied servitude to technology.

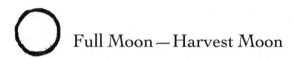 Full Moon — Harvest Moon

One of the most beautiful aspects of the European countryside, especially in Britain and Ireland, is its patchwork of irregular fields bounded by hedgerows. It is the characteristic feature of the Irish landscape viewed from an airplane, never failing to elicit gasps of delight from American tourists as their jumbo jet glides low over County Clare on its approach to Shannon Airport. It is — or once was — the most prominent aspect of the landscape viewed from the windows of our Kerry house — a crazy quilt of tiny fields, each with its own Irish name, laid out without apparent rhyme or reason but reflecting a long and exact history of land divided and divided again. Every hedgerow in Britain and Ireland is a miniature nature reserve, sheltering a rich variety of flora and fauna. Dog rose, honeysuckle, bluebell, violet, lesser celandine, hedgehog, bank vole, shrew, wood mouse, chaffinch, wren. The list is endless, with variations from place to place. Flowering hawthorn is the backbone of many hedgerows, and when it blooms in May the countryside explodes in a riot of white blossoms.

The patchwork landscape of rural Britain and Ireland has been a work in progress since the early Middle Ages, but much of it dates from about three hundred years ago, when much open land was enclosed by acts of Parliament. The new field boundaries were often banks of earth heaped up from ditches dug to either side and planted with trees and thorny shrubs that would contain animals. Hedgerows (called "ditches" in rural Ireland) were cheaper to establish than walls or fences, and they had the advantage, if properly tended, of self-renewal. With a number of small hedge-enclosed fields at his disposal, a farmer could rotate crops and animals among the fields, ensuring continued fertility. As natural habitats for wildlife, hedgerows are unsurpassed. They are ribbons of forest plaited across the landscape, a web of wilderness through which animals can move with secrecy and safety. In Britain and Ireland, hedgerows account for more acres of wildlife habitat than all nature preserves and national parks. They shelter something like a third of all species of plants and animals. Much has been written lately about the rampant destruction of tropical rain forests: the hedgerow habitats of Europe are disappearing at an equally alarming rate. Although not as significant as rain forests in the global ecology, hedgerows are nearer and dearer to the hearts of Americans because of our cultural heritage.

The pressure on hedgerows derives from the nature of modern farming. Big machinery requires big fields to operate economically. Chemical fertilizers eliminate the need to rotate crops; sustained productivity can be purchased in 110-pound plastic bags. Small unproductive farms are bought up by larger, more efficient operators, who root out hedgerows between fields, drain, and fertilize. The delightful patchwork of pastures, crops, and fallow meadows yields to an unbroken expanse of monotone green. From the farmer's point of view, the grubbing of hedgerows, as it's called, makes perfect sense. Fields can be chemically forced and mechanically harvested two or three times in a single season, without the age-old anxiety about rain-spoiled hay lost on the ground or in the stack. What is sacrificed are flowery hay meadows, the hum of insects, singing birds, and a host of other wildlife. In Britain, total hedgerow length fell from 341,000 miles in 1984 to 259,000 in 1993, a decrease of 25 percent in less than a decade. Even along the verges of public roads, where little can be gained by grubbing hedges, farmers root them out and replace them with barbed wire or electric fences, presumably to obtain a tiny extra margin of land. Country lanes that were once sun-and-shade-dappled tunnels of floral delight now might as well be on the plains of Nebraska.

Richard Muir, a noted British conservationist, has (perhaps uncharitably) described the typical hedge grubber this way: "He usually has a waxed cotton jacket, a flat tweed cap and shares his Range Rover with a dopey labrador called 'dog.' His hands are soft, his work consists of sessions with his accountant and ordering machine drivers around on a walkie-talkie . . . he is very rich and very nasty [to nature lovers and ramblers]." The hedge grubbers, on the other hand, are often quick to write off conservationists as sentimental busybodies who care more for field mice and blue-bells than for the well-being of people. Hedgerows, they remind us with some justice, are human artifacts established for economic reasons, and their destruction springs from the same motivation as their creation.

As I write, the fuchsia in the hedgerows outside my window is coming into festive bloom. Foxglove, honeysuckle, blackberry, bluebells, and wild rose add to a luxuriant palette of colors and scents. But the music of the birds and insects that live among the flowers is drowned out by the grinding moan of a huge steel-clawed machine that is grubbing hedges in fields across the way. Ultimately, the fate of the hedgerows will be decided politically. Irish farmers get government grants to grub out hedges. If the majority of the population wish to retain a visually diverse landscape that is rich in wildlife, they may have to pay for it, by subsidizing farmers to desist from grubbing. At the very least, the conservationist public should not have to pay for habitat destruction. At the present rate of grubbing, it will not be long before all of Europe's hedgerows are gone, the flowering banks and ribbons of wildwood replaced by wire, the only diversity of color that of plastic fertilizer bags piled by the side of the road.

 Last Quarter Moon

The Great Blasket Island lies a mile of so off the western coast of Ireland, just over the hill from my house in Kerry.

Until 1953, the island was home to a small, isolated community of Irish-speaking people who lived on the wrack of
shipwrecks, herrings, and potatoes, without benefit of electricity, telephones, indoor plumbing, or even that most
basic of Irish amenities, a pub. With so little in the way of
material things to sustain the life of the community, the
Blasket nevertheless produced an astonishing flowering of
fine Irish writing, including Maurice O'Sullivan's *Twenty
Years A'Growing*, Tomas O Criomhthain's *The Islandman*,
and Peig Sayers's *An Old Woman's Reflections*. Perhaps no
other acre of land has produced a more voluminous body of
literature.

The Blasket and the nearby mainland coast are places
of exceptional natural beauty, in desperate danger of overdevelopment and despoliation. The island has been acquired by the Irish government as a national park, and the
Office of Public Works has constructed an "interpretive
center" on the mainland cliffs looking out to the island. The
center is a sprawling structure that contains exhibits on island life and culture, a theater, a café, a gift shop, toilets,
and parking for dozens of cars and the huge, double-decker
tour buses that somehow manage to squeeze themselves
along West Kerry's narrow roads. Public discussion about
the building of the center was vigorous, sometimes acrimo-
nious, pitting neighbor against neighbor. I was myself mar-
ginally involved in the debate, having written a letter in the
Irish Times questioning the siting and scale of the project,
and by implication, the whole ethic of "interpretation."

Opponents believed the size and location of the center
would compromise the very thing it was meant to interpret.

Why, they asked, should tourists stand inside a building looking out at the Blasket through a plate glass window, when they could be outside on the cliffs, experiencing rock, sea, and air, as did the islanders? Let tourists who really cared about the Blasket make the crossing to the island itself, visit the tumbledown houses where the islanders lived, and feel the salt spray and the sting of the wind.

"Elitism!" cried supporters of the center. What about people who were too young, old, or infirm to make the sea crossing? What about all those folks in tour buses? Why not let them learn about Blasket culture in the comfort of a dry, warm exhibit hall, while contributing their dollars, marks, francs, and pounds to the local economy?

The battle over Blasket Island was decided in favor of building, but the same battle is being fought all over Ireland. The Office of Public Works has built or wants to build interpretive centers in the heart of the limestone Burren, the Wicklow Mountains, and other places of exceptional natural beauty or historical interest. Ironically, both sides in these emotionally charged battles consider themselves environmentalists. The Office of Public Works believes it is discharging its responsibility to preserve and enhance the national heritage, opening areas of natural beauty to wider public appreciation. Opponents of the centers believe the fragile environments of these places are already severely stressed by overuse. The final straw, they say, will be long lines of tour buses disgorging hordes of tourists who want nothing more than postcards, cheap souvenirs, and a trip to the loo.

These battles in Ireland are skirmishes in a global war

between preservationists and advocates of public access. Do airplane flights within the walls of the Grand Canyon provide the public with an unparalleled experience of nature, or does the roar of the engines destroy the silent essence of the canyon's beauty? How many raft trips down the Colorado River are consistent with the canyon's wilderness character? How many tourists can enter Yosemite Valley or Yellowstone National Park before those places are awash in sewage, exhaust fumes, and litter? Do all-terrain vehicles and snowmobiles facilitate access to wilderness, or do they obviate the wilderness experience? Who has a right to experience wilderness—only sensitive environmental types with trendy anoraks and fanny packs, or the teeming masses?

I will confess that my heart sank when I saw the hulk of the Blasket Island Interpretive Center rising on a stretch of cliffs so beautiful and unspoiled that it was used as a setting for the films *Ryan's Daughter* and *Far and Away.* On the other hand, when the center was finished, my first visit there was strangely moving; from the inside, it seemed altogether appropriate that the extraordinary folk culture of the island should be celebrated in photographs, stories, models, and artifacts. As a person of democratic principles, I would hesitate to deny anyone access to natural beauty, I applaud the celebration of folk literature, and I respect the fact that a majority of local opinion was in favor of building the center. At the same time, I know that something precious and irreplaceable has been lost. The battle over the Blasket Island Interpretive Center was fraught with all that is complex and difficult in the ongoing war between public access and preservation. It is a war that cannot be resolved to everyone's satisfaction.

Nevertheless, sooner or later we all must take a stand. Until his death in 1953, Ireland's preeminent naturalist, Robert Lloyd Praeger, visited every corner of the nation, cataloging its rocks, plants, animals, and archaeological riches. He traveled "mostly on foot, sometimes by cycle, seldom by car," for that, he said, is the only way to know intimately any country. His account of his travels, *The Way That I Went*, affirms the value of "stopping often, watching closely, listening carefully"—in short, what I have called here natural prayer.

New England

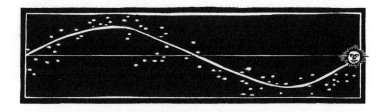

Autumn Equinox

 New Moon

My field guide calls the cardinal flower "bright red." Those words inadequately describe the flower's electric presence in the ditch. Scarlet? Vermilion? No, not nearly enough pizzazz. Let's call in the people who invent the names on paint chips. Valentine red. Stoplight red. Chili Pepper red. Red Ridinghood red. No other New England wildflower is so conspicuously colored. Thoreau referred to the cardinal flower's "red artillery." On another occasion he was reminded of "the scarlet of sin."

I've been watching a particular colony of cardinal flowers for a dozen years, one of only two colonies I know about in our neighborhood. Its population has modestly waxed and waned, sometimes teetering on the brink of local extinction. It is near a path trod by many young people who probably cannot resist picking the flowers. Two years ago I counted sixteen plants spread out along fifty feet of drainage ditch; the next year only three; this year six. In his journal, Thoreau describes a ditch clogged with the plants, ten to the square foot, four or five thousand in all, like an advancing rank of redcoats. My colony is more ragtag, like a shattered troop of British regulars straggling home from defeat at Lexington. Still, it enlivens the late summer with its flintlock flash of crimson. The cardinal flower is a North American native. Early explorers of the continent admired the plant and shipped it home to France and England, where it became a garden favorite. The genus designator of its Latin name, *Lobelia cardinalis*, derives from the Flemish botanist Matthias de Lobel. The Lobel family name came from the white poplar or "abele" tree, so we have a name migrating from a plant to a human family and back again to a plant. *Cardinalis*, of course, refers to the color worn by princes of the Roman Catholic Church. Blue is a more common color among our late-summer wildflowers; yellow and white are even more ubiquitous. Still, as Thoreau noted, a little *cardinalis* goes a long way. My handful of crimson plants announce their presence from far off, standing out among their massed green neighbors with princely ostentation.

For plants, green is the color of livelihood. The green pigment in plants is chlorophyll, a chemical that harnesses sunlight and channels its energy into substances that provide food for all life. For plants, green is nine-to-five, nose-to-the-grindstone, earning one's keep. Red, on the other hand, is the color of reproduction, and from the gaudy, party-hat look of it, the cardinal flower appears to be having fun. With pools of nectar at the base of deep-throated blossoms, the cardinal flower, like the wild columbine, is adapted to pollination by long-beaked hummingbirds and daytime moths with extended mouthparts. I've never seen a hummingbird or moth near my colony, but someone must be visiting; the plants somehow hang on, year after year. The cardinal flower's blossom rivals the lady's slipper for ingenious design, although a magnifier is helpful for inspecting the reproductive apparatus. Perfectly positioned above each nectar-filled tube is an overhanging flower part that goes through two stages, first male, then female. As a hummingbird or moth arrives to feed at a flower in the male stage, its forehead is dusted with pollen by a little white brush. When it goes to feed at a flower in the female stage, the pollen is wiped off by a sticky purple pad. The cardinal flower needs winged creatures to bring pollen and eggs together; hummingbirds and moths need the cardinal flower's stores of solar energy. It's a trade-off: I'll scratch your back and you scratch mine. We're all part of it, this web of interdependence, up to our necks in it. Climatologists insist that the stability of our weather depends upon maintaining the present balance of plants and animals. Geologists tell us that the air we breathe is the delicate exhalation of a seamless web of life. No species is expendable; we are bound together by our mutual need. But sometimes it takes a kick in the head to make the depth of the interdependence sink in—like observing with a magnifier that little pollen-tipped brush of the male cardinal flower and the sticky pad of the female flower, contrived by millions of years of evolution to exploit the forehead of a moth.

Of course, not all plants require birds or insects to complete their sexual transactions. For hundreds of millions of years, plants relied almost exclusively upon wind and water to unite the male and female germs, with perhaps some catch-as-catch-can pollination by animals. Then, about 100 million years ago, in the Cretaceous period—not so long ago on the geologic timescale—plants evolved advertising, colored blossoms shouting "Here I am!" Fossils tell the story: suddenly, magnolias are blooming among cone-bearing pines and flowering sassafras among the ferns, bright-hued additions to a world of green. Like fur and feathers, the idea of blossoms seems obvious once we have it, but who could have imagined it before the fact? It's no accident that we are so powerfully drawn to the cardinal flowers strung out along the ditch. The whole point of their "see-me" color is to attract attention, a purpose perhaps not altogether different from that of their scarlet-clad ecclesiastical eponyms. Of course, it is not us they are trying to attract; our dietary needs and mouthparts are not adapted to spreading pollen. For that they need hummingbirds or moths also drawn to siren-screaming blossoms of Fire Engine red.

 First Quarter Moon

There is nothing ostentatious about Indian pipes. If the cardinal flower goes in for screaming "See me," the Indian pipe

has opted for the life of a colorless scavenger, eschewing
even the green of honest livelihood. In late September they
are common in our pine-oak woods, pushing up through the
leaf litter of the forest floor, little covens of waxy-white
wildflowers, ghostly, bewitching, vaguely demonic. Corpse
plant, ghost flower, ice plant: the Indian pipe's common
names convey that same spooky, cold-as-death impression.
No gaudy petals, not a tinge of chlorophyll—the Indian
pipe simply doesn't fit our idea of what a wildflower should
be. The casual observer might mistake the plant for a fungus, some sort of bulb-capped mushroom casting spores on
the wind. But it is a true wildflower, a seed-producing vas-
cular plant, almost unique among our common plants in
that it has no hint of green. Colorless in every part, or perhaps with a hint of pink in the flower head, Indian pipes
lack the pigment that enables other wildflowers to absorb
energy from sunlight. It must therefore live off food produced by other plants. Like mushrooms, it derives its sustenance from decaying vegetable matter. In place of the usual
root system, the Indian pipe maintains a cozy underground
relationship with a fungus. The fungus assists the plant by
breaking down organic matter in the soil. In a sense, the
Indian pipe is a parasite on a parasite, twice removed from
the light of the sun. It is this independence of sunlight that
allows the plant to thrive in shadows.

These spectral parasitical plants have inspired in their
beholders a dark range of sentiments. A typical reaction
can be found in Neltje Blanchan's book on wildflowers
from early in this century. From the wraithlike Indian pipe

Blanchan draws a turgid moral tale. The plant, she writes, stands as a branded sinner: "Doubtless its ancestors were industrious, honest creatures, seeking their food with good green matter [chlorophyll] on which virtuous vegetative life depends; but some ancestral knave elected to live by piracy, to drain the already-food of its neighbors." So far, Blanchan is on the mark. The Indian pipe is a member of the wintergreen family of plants, not far removed from the heaths, and therefore a relative of such woodland favorites as rhododendron, azalea, and laurel—sturdy, honest creatures all. How botanists manage to find much in common between the colorless, parasitical Indian pipes and those glossy-green, flower-bedecked shrubs must seem a mystery, a bit of voodoo taxonomy. But sure enough, in spite of their superficial dissimilarities, all of these plants share certain defining characteristics—radially symmetric flowers, superior ovaries, four or five petals usually fused, fruit a capsule or berry, and so forth. It is easier to see a likeness between Indian pipe and its smallish cousins of the woodland floor, the wintergreen and the pipsissewa, but even here the resemblance is like that between a living, breathing human being and a zombie. The Indian pipe has surrendered its color. Its leaves have degenerated into scaly bracts. Blanchan says it is no wonder this backslider hangs its head; it is no wonder it grows black with shame on being picked, as if its wickedness were only then discovered. She finds only one thing to admire in the Indian pipe: "When the minute, innumerable seeds begin to form, it proudly raises its head erect, as if conscious that it had performed the one righteous act of its life." Thoreau was perhaps more charitable in seeing a clump of Indian pipes as a gathering of maidens, robed in pure white, nurtured in a dark underground cloister, and now making their entrance into a world of light. Under their white hoods and capes (writes Thoreau) the virtuous sisters strive to conceal their nakedness and tenderness. But soon, exposed to light and air, their virtue is turned black. Thoreau's image is accurate. Once fertilized, the nodding white flower of the Indian pipe becomes erect and the plant becomes tough and black. The capsule at the top of the mature plant splits down the sides and the seeds are spilled to the wind.

We smile at the way early nature writers like Thoreau and Blanchan discovered moral lessons among the creatures of the forest floor. But the bizarre biology of Indian pipes seems to call for the flamboyant metaphor. Their whiteness begs for a generous helping of purple prose. Ghouls, phantoms, ectoplasmic spooks: these are the words that come to mind. But the plant hardly deserves its reputation as grave robber and spook. It is surely no more or less despicable than any other wildflower parasite—pinesap, beech drops, broomrape or dodder—and has its own claim to our affection. In this day when the recycling of wastes and the frugal use of energy resources are considered honorable activities, the Indian pipe cannot be faulted for squeezing a modest living out of the squandered residue of summer. "In summer, greenness is cheap," said Thoreau. Plants with chlorophyll can afford to be spendthrifts. The Indian pipe is nature's way of pinching pennies.

O Full Moon — Hunter's Moon

October blows through New England like a hurricane of color. Chlorophyll in the leaves of deciduous trees breaks down, and other pigments — anthocyanins and carotenoids — come to the fore. Charles Darwin took note of the autumnal display that makes New England famous: "The tints of the decaying leaves in an American forest are described by everyone as gorgeous; yet no one supposes that these tints are of the least advantage to trees." He raised the question of how color fits into evolution. October's riot is apparently an accident, an exercise in useless ostentation on the part of the trees, an embarrassment to evolutionists who like to find a reason for everything. The crimson splurge of autumnal maples is superfluous, like the red of arterial blood, which, according to Darwin, "adds to the beauty of the maiden's cheek, but no one will pretend that it has been acquired for that purpose." October is a gorgeous but meaningless extravaganza — at least from the evolutionist's point of view.

Why are the things in nature the colors that they are? You may have heard the rhyme: "I never saw a purple cow, I hope to never see one; But I will tell you, anyhow, I'd rather see than be one." So why *aren't* cows purple? Or pink? The cardinal flower has an incentive to announce its presence to the hummingbird, but what advantage accrues to the hummingbird from a gaudy iridescence that would seem to make it more conspicuous to predators? The standard answer for the hummingbird has to do with sexual

display—attracting a mate. But some other riddles of coloration are difficult to answer. The biologist Ralph Lewin
once asked in the journal *Nature,* "Why are cows not
green?" His question is not altogether frivolous. Sometimes
apparently silly questions can have interesting answers.

Lewin's question was sparked by a report in *Nature* by
Diane Stoecker, Ann Michaels, and Linda Davis, biologists
at the Woods Hole Oceanographic Institution. These researchers studied some remarkable little animals that use
sunlight to make food. But wait! you say. Animals can't do
that. Only plants have the necessary chemical machinery
for photosynthesis. Indeed, the ability to make food from
sunlight is the defining characteristic of plants. Plant cells
have little compartments called chloroplasts that contain
chlorophyll. It is chlorophyll that gives plants their characteristic green color. And chlorophyll enables plants to use
the energy of sunlight to build sugars and other nutritious
things. Animal cells have no chloroplasts. So animals must
get their energy by eating plants, or by eating other animals
that eat plants. With one exception! The animals studied by
the Woods Hole scientists are single-celled, microscopic
protozoa that live in the sea. These single-celled animals
graze upon algae, single-celled plants, much as a cow might
graze upon grass. And here's the rub. The protozoa digest
most of the substance of the algae, but not the chloroplasts,
the parts of the alga cell that are involved in photosynthesis.
The microscopic animals then use these commandeered
plant parts to make their own energy from sunlight. In a
sense, these tricky protozoa are animals that do a bit of
gardening *inside* their own bodies. The chlorophyll in the

borrowed chloroplasts gives these otherwise transparent and colorless animals a distinctly greenish tinge.

So, asks Lewin, why don't cows do the same thing? Cows eat grass. Why don't cows retain intact the chloroplasts from the grass cells? They could then do a bit of photosynthesis on the inside, making some of their own food directly rather than wasting all that time grazing on grass. A little carbon dioxide from the air, a little water, a few rays from the sun, and—voilà!—self-made dinner, already inside ready for use. The reason that cows aren't green, says Lewin, is because their digestive tracts are too clumsy for this delicate sort of recycling—that is, digesting the cellular protoplasm without harming the chloroplasts. And, besides, cows are too bulky and too opaque for ingested chloroplasts to have access to sunlight. What works for a tiny, transparent protozoa would never work in an animal as big and as opaque as a cow.

OK, so cows can't recycle chloroplasts. But, says Philip Stewart of Oxford University, the question of why there are no green cows can be generalized: Why are there no green mammals? Field mice? Tigers? Elephants? Green is the optimal color for camouflage in grasslands and forests. And there is nothing impossible about green pigmentation: there are plenty of green birds, reptiles, and amphibians. It would seem that natural selection should have favored at least a few green mammals. Maybe, muses Stewart, mammals inherit their colors from drab, mostly nocturnal ancestors. But protective coloration has a high survival value. It does not seem unreasonable that green squirrels, green cows, or even green humans might have evolved in a world dominated by green plants. It is odd that tens of millions of years of evolution have failed to produce green animals that are active in daylight.

But let's not stop here. Why is green the dominant color of terrestrial plants? That's easy. Chlorophyll molecules absorb light at the red and blue ends of the spectrum. It is the middle of the spectrum (the green part) that is reflected and gives plants their characteristic color. A more efficient photosynthetic pigment would be black, absorbing all colors, soaking up all the energy of sunlight, reflecting nothing. The reflected green light of plants is wasted energy. So perhaps the real question is, Why isn't grass black? Andrew Goldsworthy, a biologist at the Imperial College in London, has a possible answer. He draws our attention to certain purple bacteria that live in salt lakes, called *Halobacterium halobium*. This particular microbe accomplishes a very primitive sort of photosynthesis using a pigment other than chlorophyll that absorbs light in the middle (green) part of the spectrum. This leaves red and blue light at opposite ends of the spectrum to be reflected and gives the bacteria their purple color. Goldsworthy believes this sort of microbe was the earliest form of life on Earth, teeming in great numbers in the earliest seas. Chlorophyll-using bacteria evolved later (according to Goldsworthy) and were forced to make use of the light falling on the sea that wasn't already soaked up by the initially more numerous purple bacteria. These later, green bacteria were ultimately more successful, chemically speaking, and soon overwhelmed their purple cousins. And from the green bacteria evolved all green plants. Most of this is pure speculation on the part of Goldsworthy, but it raises the intriguing possibility that except for a fluke of evolution plants might have descended from *H. halobium*, the purple photosynthesizer. In which case, we might today have purple grass. And, as a corollary, protectively colored purple mammals. So the question, Why are there no purple cows? is not so silly after all. But I will tell you anyhow, I'd rather see than be one.

 Last Quarter Moon

Migrant birds fly south, deciduous trees turn technicolor and then drop their leaves, wildflowers fade. But for the woods walker, late autumn offers one welcome boon: silence. Trail bikes and all-terrain vehicles are mostly put away, and it is too early for snowmobiles. For a few blessed weeks the woods are relatively free of the sound of internal combustion. There are certain woodsy sounds that can only be heard in the complete absence of technological noise: the papery shiver of beech leaves, the ethereal whir of mourning doves rising from the ground, the rattle of wild indigo seedpods when stirred by the wind. The range of human hearing can be represented as a graph of sound intensity versus frequency. The lower bound of the range is called the threshold of hearing: for example, at the frequency of the chickadee's call (2,800 vibrations per second), a sound must have an intensity of about 5 decibels to be heard at all. The upper limit of the range of audibility is called the threshold of pain. At the frequency of middle C (256 vibrations per second), the limit of pain has an intensity of about 130 decibels, or only slightly greater than the sound of a snowmobile engine at close range. I like to think of the graph of human audibility as a blank canvas upon which nature paints with sound. To hear the tapping of a nuthatch requires a soundscape that is mostly free of background noise. The roar of a trail bike or snowmobile is equivalent to throwing a bucket of black paint onto the ear's white canvas. It was in an essay titled "Sounds" that Thoreau made his well-known remark about needing "a broad margin to my life." This is the time of the year when woods walkers have the broadest margin to their aural sense, when the relative absence of recreational machines provides the ear with a wide expanse of quiet onto which nature can sketch marginal notes of subtle sound.

Two sounds of autumn are unmistakable, says naturalist Hal Borland: "The hurrying rustle of crisp leaves blown along the street or road by gusty wind, and the gabble of a flock of migrating geese." To these he might have added the sound that epitomizes the New England autumn: the *tunk-tunk* of acorns falling from oaks. Squirrels are up there playing Tarzan among the branches of the trees, and down comes the shower of acorns, bouncing off the leaf litter on the forest floor. The squirrels, it seems, are enjoying a last boisterous fling before gathering the harvest. And why not? There's plenty of acorns to go around. The ground is littered with them. According to Indian lore, a rich crop of acorns means we are in for a hard winter. If so, then nature has a generous way of anticipating the rigor of the coming season. Squirrels stash away acorns in huge numbers as

winter reserves, often burying them in the ground and for-
getting where they put them. The buried acorns are in
perfect position for germinating the following spring, protected from the winter freeze by a few inches of soil. In
his *Guide to Nature in Winter,* Donald Stokes suggests that
many of our northern oaks have grown up from squirrel-
forgotten acorn caches.

Birds — ruffed grouse, blue jay, nuthatch, titmouse — eat
acorns, pecking open the shell and gobbling the nut. Wild
turkeys gulp down acorns, shells and all, dozens in a single
meal. Bear, deer, and raccoons, too, depend on acorns in
winter. Donald Stokes observes that no other tree provides
so much food for so many as do oaks. Acorns are probably
our wildlife's most important source of sustenance. Humans
eat them, too, usually after lots of boiling, but sometimes
right off the ground. I've nibbled acorns and found them
decidedly unpalatable, which is why I'm always surprised
that Thoreau goes on so in his journals about their culinary
advantages. The hermit of Walden is positively rhapsodic
about the sweet taste of acorns. You would think he was
talking about French truffles or Italian chocolates. It's
white-oak acorns he's talking about, the least bitter of these
bitter fruits. "To my taste, they are quite as good as chest-
nuts," says Thoreau, professing to prefer them to a slice of
imported pineapple. "Their sweetness is like the sweetness
of bread." Can he possibly be talking about the same acorns
I've tasted? In an unguarded moment in his journal,
Thoreau admits that acorns, like wild apples, require an
"outdoor appetite." Apparently, when he tried them in the
house, they were not so pineapple-tasty. Then, catching

himself out of character, he quickly adds, "Is not the out-door appetite the one to be prayed for?"

Well, I don't know that it is. Here's an outdoorsy recipe to add to your collection. It's from a book called *Wanderings of an Artist* by Paul Kane, published in 1859. Kane spent four years traveling thousands of miles across Canada, recording in his sketchbook the lives and habits of Native Americans. Among the Chinook Indians he observed the following practice: "About a bushel of acorns are placed in a hole dug for the purpose close to the entrance of the lodge or hut, covered over with a thin layer of grass, on top of which is laid about half a foot of earth. Every member of the family henceforth regards this hole as the special place of deposit for his urine, which is on no occasion to be di-verted from its legitimate receptacle. In this hole the acorns are allowed to remain four or five months before they are considered fit for use. . . . The product is regarded by them as the greatest of all delicacies." Chinook olives: that's what European explorers called this treat. Kane's tale may of-fend fastidious modern sensibilities, but the Chinook way of treating acorns served a purpose. Acorns have long been an important foodstuff in many parts of the world, includ-ing Mexico and Europe, but only after the tannic acid has been leached from the nuts. For Native Americans this usu-ally meant burying the acorns underground for long peri-ods of time or suspending them in running water. A bath of urine apparently helps.

During their first hungry winter in Massachusetts, the Pilgrims were lucky to find baskets of acorns the Indians had buried in the ground. Those buried nuts may have been a lifesaver, but as soon as they could the Pilgrims switched to another Indian treat—turkey with all the trimmings—and never looked back. Some modern epicures claim to relish acorns, and handbooks of edible wild plants contain lots of allegedly delicious acorn recipes. Thoreau tells us that after an acorn snack he felt like he possessed "the heart and back of oak." Maybe so, but the crunch of acorns underfoot doesn't whet my appetite. Nibbling a white oak acorn on a brisk autumn day may have a certain derring-do charm, but these days no one wants to live on them, and certainly not prepared in the Chinook way. The fruits of oaks may please the palates of squirrels and hermits, but most of us will settle for the sweet *tunk-tunk* of autumn's most characteristic sound.

 New Moon

On crisp autumn mornings the meadow is a universe of galaxies: spiderwebs made visible by dew. Starstrung spirals suspended on glistening threads. Tangled silk mats in the grass. Silver funnels, with a spider waiting at each funnel's black throat. This is architecture for the belly, silken snares set for dinner. "What refinement of art for a mess of flies!" exclaimed the great entomologist Jean-Henri Fabre, in his *Life of the Spider.* "Nowhere, in the whole animal kingdom, has the need to eat inspired a more cunning industry." It is worth getting up early to see the perfection of the spider's work, before wind, rain, birds, and insects wreak their destruction. While we sleep, the virtuosos of silk are busy. Flinging gossamer strands across the void. Repairing the porches of their burrows. Extending sticky tablecloth traps. And, most spectacularly, spinning spiral webs against the sky.

The spinning of silk is the spider's greatest accomplishment, a tour de force of evolution. Spiders are born with the weaver's talent. Hatchlings spin webs that rival the finest works of adults. Says Fabre, "There are no masters or apprentices in their guild; all know their craft from the moment that the first thread is laid." According to one popular hypothesis, web building had its origin in the silky line that all spiders play out behind them wherever they go. Originally, the line served only to help the spider find its way home. But after many forays, the mass of threads near the entrance to the spider's shelter proved useful for another purpose: if an insect touched the sheet of resonant silk, the spider was alerted by vibration, and the prey was soon secured. From this accidental doormat, so the story goes, all future webs evolved. This happened quite some time ago. Fossil spiders with spinnerets (silk glands) on their abdomens are known from the Devonian and Carboniferous periods, 300 to 400 million years ago. Fossil silk is not preserved, so we do not yet know when spiders first built webs. Indirect evidence suggests that by the early Cretaceous, 100 million years ago, web building was well advanced. Paleontologist Paul Selden of Manchester University has found richly detailed fossil spiders from 100-million-year-old limestone of northeastern Spain, almost photographic in quality, that clearly show claws adapted for handling silk and for locomotion on spiral webs. The same limestone contains abundant insect fossils, evidence for ample spider prey. Even then, apparently, in the time of the dinosaurs, spiders spun traps of exquisite delicacy—and flourished.

Across millions of years, spiders refined and diversified their craft. A garden spider can manufacture as many as eight types of silk, each especially suited for its purpose. Web silk, for example, is different from the silks used for egg sacs and or binding prey. The familiar orb web of a garden spider consists of two types of silk. The threads radiating from the center are stiff and nonsticky; they provide a strong scaffolding for the web. The circular threads, or capture threads, are elastic and studded with glue droplets; they hold insects fast and stretch without breaking. As a spider spins the capture threads it coats the silk with a viscous liquid. Surface tension causes the liquid to contract into droplets, the way a thin stream of water from a faucet breaks up into drops. As the drops coalesce along the thread, some of the silk is gathered up in bunches within the drops. When the thread is stretched, the silk unwinds from the droplets, like tiny key chains on spring-loaded reels, and then pulls back tight into the drops. It is a device wonderfully suited for holding insects with virtually unbreakable bonds. In experiments performed by Fritz Vollrath and Donald Edmonds of Oxford University, capture threads were contracted to a twentieth of their length in the web without sagging, and stretched to three times their length without breaking. If human engineers could reproduce these astonishing properties in thread or cable of a larger size, it would be the greatest product to hit the market since nylon.

We often hear it said that science takes the wonder and mystery out of nature. And it is true, I suppose, that reports of discoveries of spider fossils and experiments on spider silk can make dreary reading in the scientific literature; like all scientific reports, they are couched in technical language and full of tedious numbers and diagrams. But the information contained in the reports certainly enhances our appreciation for the spider's craft. The silky galaxies in the morning meadow seem even more miraculous when we know the properties of the silk, the subtlety of the engineering, and the history of the weaver's craft. Here, in dozens of glistening webs, the spider composes symphonies of silk. Swiveling spinnerets move in concert with agile claws, devising, measuring, laying down lines, practicing an art learned in the company of dinosaurs, perfected in the planet's first grassy meadows, and communicated across tens of millions of generations by the ineluctable agency of genes.

 First Quarter Moon

Woolly bears are on the march. Double time. Making tracks. Trucking. They really move, along the sidewalk, across the path, at a typical speed of one yard per minute — supersonic for a caterpillar — on sixteen little legs (or what pass for legs) hidden in their brushy fur. Where are they going in such a tizzy? The guidebooks say that if you see a woolly bear on the path in the fall, it is looking for a secure place to spend the winter—under leaves, inside a log, behind a loose clapboard of the house. Then why do we so often see them on open paths, barreling along in the same direction we are going, as if late for an appointment or taking a jog? Of course, they'll get to their hibernation places sooner or later. I've occasionally found them in January or February curled up under leaves or logs like sleeping kittens, snoozing the winter away in frozen slumber. The naturalist Edwin Way Teale described the tightly curled woolly bears as "dozing doughnuts." But the search for a suitable wintering place doesn't seem to explain the caterpillar's October predilection for sidewalks, roads, and open spaces. Even a half-blind bug with a pinpoint brain can tell smooth asphalt from a place that is likely to have cozy nooks and crannies. I'll tell you what the woolly bears are doing. They are doing the same thing we are doing. Enjoying the last warm days of autumn. Taking the air. Stretching their limbs.

Anyone who has become jaded with life, forgetful of mystery, or merely bored with the natural world, should pick up a woolly bear caterpillar and place it in the palm of his hand. An inch and a half of slippery fur. A walking mustache. Two bulging eyes (or what look like eyes) among the bristles, the only way to tell which end is going and which is coming. This fragile slip of cuteness—for, yes, they are cute, a favorite pet of children, worthy of a place in the teddy bear stores—survives New England's deep freeze, one of the hardy insects that winter over in the vulnerable larval stage (as opposed to the hardier egg stage). In spring, it wakes, has a bite to eat, then rolls itself into a pupa, using its woolly hairs to make a cocoon, lashing them together with self-produced silk. Two weeks later, an Isabella tiger moth emerges—*presto-chango*, a magician's trick. A black-and-brown woolly bear goes into the box—a wave of the wand—a yellow-winged tiger moth emerges. Somehow, the creature has managed to remake itself, rearranging its molecules, from a crawling fuzzball into an airborne angel. In few other insects is the miracle of metamorphosis so stunning, so complete. A crawling, insatiable, leaf-eating machine is transformed into a winged, sex-obsessed nectar sipper. Shape, color, internal organs, mode of transport— all utterly changed. It's as if an elephant became a swan, or a rattlesnake became a parakeet.

Of course, the totality of the transformation is to some extent illusory. What remains constant through all the stages of metamorphosis is information. It's all there, at the heart of every cell, in the DNA blueprints for making a woolly bear caterpillar and a tiger moth. There are clusters of cells in the larval caterpillar that are destined to become anatomical features of the adult moth, dormant, awaiting a chemical signal that will make them surge into activity. The warmth of spring releases hormones from glands in or near the caterpillar's brain. These cause the woolly bear to build a chrysalis and begin metamorphosis. Previously dormant adult cells begin to multiply. They take their nutrients from superseded larval cells, which are transformed into a kind of nutrient soup for the benefit of the growing adult organs.

The woolly bear's six stumpy front feet are turned into the tiger moth's slender legs. Four bright wings develop, as do reproductive organs. Chewing mouthparts become adapted for sucking. In two weeks, the remaking is complete. The chrysalis breaks.

There is no way to think about these things without gasping for breath. It's one thing to understand the biology, at least that part of it that we know something about: DNA, hormones, gene expression, and all that. But knowing the biology only makes the metamorphosis all the more breathtaking. Not magic, but what the poet Mary Oliver calls "the light at the center of every cell," permeating every atom of matter, soaking nature the way water soaks a sponge. What is it? It is easy to recognize life when we see it, but devilishly hard to say what it is. Half a century ago the great Austrian physicist Erwin Schrödinger wrote a book called *What Is Life?* He was convinced that life would eventually be accounted for by physics and chemistry, and his book helped inspire the biomolecular revolution, but the best he could do for a definition was "an elaborate, coherent, meaningful design traced by the great master." More recently, the American biologist Lynn Margulis and her son Dorion Sagan tackled the question again in a book of the same title: *What Is Life?* They provide a brilliant summary of what we have learned about life—the biochemistry and cellular organization—but the sought-for definition remains elusive. Margulis and Sagan try their hand at several definitions: "It is a material process, sifting and surfing over matter like a strange, slow wave . . . the watery, membrane-bound encapsulation of spacetime . . . a planetary exuberance . . . existence's celebration." All of which are lovely metaphors, but none of which gets us any closer to the ineluctable heart of the mystery. Call it simply life, call it God, call it an inch and a half of black-and-brown fur. It can't be ignored when you hold it curled in your hand, a gram of divinity.

Lift the woolly bear gently from your palm, taking care not to let it slip between your fingers. Place it again on the sidewalk. The larva of the Isabella tiger moth slowly uncurls, lifts its head (ah, so *that's* the front end), takes a near-sighted gaze around (or is it a sniff?), then scurries off in its headlong dash for who-knows-what, a many-footed distillation of the Heraclitean fire that animates the world, hell-bent-for-caterpillar-leather under October's golden sun.

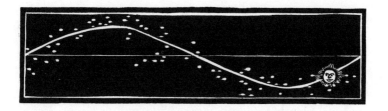

Halloween

 Full Moon — Frosty Moon

A fabulous autumn for mushrooms. More mushrooms than I can ever remember, particularly impressive after last year's drought. In the woods, in the meadows, near the garden paths. A Halloween bounty of fungal spooks, dining on the detritus of summer. A cool wet summer prepared the earth. Autumn rains tease them out of the ground. Ghosts, wraiths, imps, and specters: they appear at night, as if evoked by incantations, then fade in the sun. A goblin market. Nature's trick-or-treaters.

On decaying wood chips at the side of a path, I find a cluster of—what? They look like small starfish. Three or four bumpy arms uplifted, tips touching. Coral pink. Are they alive? I pick one from the chips, place it in the palm of my hand. It looks like a live animal. The texture of living flesh. But the stench! A stench of death. It is a mushroom, of course, unlike any I have seen before. Clearly in the stinkhorn family. It has the cadaverous stinkhorn odor that attracts flies that feed on the sticky spores massed along the "starfish" arms. The flies become covered with spores and spread the fungus far and wide. A mushroom handbook reveals the name: Stinky Squid. Perfect! Turn it upside down and the arms dangle from a bulbous body, squidlike.

Late October. Green fades. Chlorophyll closes down. This is the season of the Grim Reaper. Mushrooms skulk the forest floor like cursed spirits costumed for mischief, the spectral garb of Pandemonium. Here is another mushroom I haven't seen in our woods before, in Draculian clusters by the path. Funereal purple. Shaped like trumpets. Horns of Plenty, they are called in my handbook. The French more appropriately call them "Trumpets of the Dead." Why do so many species of mushrooms have Halloween names? Destroying angel. Fairy helmets. Jack-o'-lanterns. Death cap. Witches' butter. The names betray our feelings. We don't trust mushrooms. Something deep in our folk consciousness turns away in revulsion. Is it that some of them are poisonous? Hallucinogenic? Or is it something deeper? Something druidical? Are we reminded of the fairy spirits of our forest-living European ancestors? Is this what Shakespeare's Prospero had in mind when he addressed the elves "whose pastime is to make midnight mushrooms"?

Fungi are heterotrophs, which means they require for their nourishment organic compounds synthesized by other organisms, namely, green plants. Some fungi are parasites: they take nutrients from a living host. Most fungi are saprobes: they obtain nutrients from nonliving organic matter and cause its decay. What we familiarly know as mushrooms are actually the short-lived fruiting bodies of a fungus, like apples on a tree. The living organism, called the mycelium, is a web of branching fibers hidden within decaying matter, threads so fine as to be individually almost invisible, but cobwebby white when seen en masse. The mycelium secretes digestive enzymes, which break down organic matter, and then absorbs the products. Since the digestive reaction takes place outside the fungal cells, living plants can also benefit from the released nutrients. The reaction generates carbon dioxide, also of use to plants. It has been said that the world would be a heap of old rubbish if it were not for the mushrooms and their ability to get rid of it. That's not quite true. Heterotrophic bacteria do their part in ridding us of the detritus of death. But it is certainly true that mushrooms play an indispensable role in recycling the materials of life, in balancing the great chemical equations of earth and atmosphere.

Mushrooms are the grave robbers of the plant world, shunners of sunlight, and it is appropriate that they come out in autumn's failing light to skulk with goblins, witches, incubi, and succubi, dancing in fairy circles. There is something darkly sexual about them. The phallic stinkhorn. The vulval earthstar. And those wicked little men of the woods, which I have never seen except in foreign handbooks, the crowned earthstars, *Geastrum fornicatum,* marching in lascivious gangs, with open mouths. Our ancestors roaming the dark forests of northern Europe may have seen the mushrooms as spirits of the dead in macabre resurrection. Appearing overnight, in garish colors, these Lords of the Flies evoke, somehow, mysteriously, thoughts of malevolence and lust. We have inherited from that time a poetry of names that invests mushrooms with an aspect of evil rivaled only by that which we associate with snakes.

Mushrooms are bearers of myth and magic, icons of mortality. They are also nature's recyclers, fascinating in their curious forms, in their colorful comings and goings. "Here is beauty from decay," wrote the naturalist Edwin Way Teale, "a frail and insubstantial form of life, a kind of botanical ectoplasm." So bring on the ghostbusters. This year's mushrooms have been bigger, more colorful, more numerous, and more varied than ever, excited to a witches' Sabbath by frequent rain. And this is their week, their final fling—night-stalking tricksters, ectoplasmic Halloween spooks.

 Last Quarter Moon

A still November morning. Brittle, transparent, like glass. Suddenly shattered. Not fifty feet away, a huge bird labors into the air, with a gray burden in its talons. Push, push, push—gaining altitude. It comes to rest on the branch of a pine. A red-tailed hawk. I slip my binoculars from my shoulder bag and focus. The hawk appears to be sitting upon a plump cushion of feathers. I move closer, keeping my glasses on the bird, until I see that the cushion is a pigeon, not dead, but terrified into stillness. I am witnessing something primal, unpretty, true—nature red in tooth and claw—the bloody engine of evolution that drives life, creates beauty, contrives complexity. Beauty and terror: the twin faces of nature.

A few days later I am in Washington, D.C., visiting the National Gallery of Art's exhibit of John James Audubon's watercolors for his great folio collection *Birds of America.* Here among a peaceable kingdom of warblers, vireos, and wrens are Audubon's red-tailed hawks, male and female, caught by the artist's brush in midair, the male's wings swept back, his talons tearing at the female, seeking to snatch from her the frightened hare in her claws. The painting was done in Louisiana in 1821, not long after Audubon witnessed the airborne battle. The postures of the birds show their plumage to best ornithological advantage. We are given the male bird's back, the female's breast. The beaks are rendered in profile and from the top. The red tail feathers are shown from above and below. It was Audubon's genius that he was able to combine lively storytelling with accurate scientific description. It is the source of our enduring fascination with his art.

Audubon refused to prettify nature or soften its apparent cruelty. The hare in the female's talons can almost be seen to shiver and whimper with fright. Its belly is streaked with blood and urine. This harsh realism is also part of our fascination with Audubon. When the artist arrived in Edinburgh, Scotland, looking for a printer for his work, he showed his watercolors to the engraver William Home Lizars. Lizars was immediately drawn especially to the paintings depicting violence in nature: mockingbirds attacked by a rattlesnake, a hawk pouncing on seventeen partridges, and a whooping crane eating newborn alligators.

The engraver decided to begin his work with Audubon's great-footed hawks, "with bloody rags at their beaks' ends and cruel delight in their daring eyes."

Audubon was a woodsman. He shot birds to paint them. He experienced daily the hard continuum of violence that links us with other beasts. He also participated in several incidents of gratuitous violence of a kind that separates humankind from the rest of nature. In Kentucky, in 1813, a billion passenger pigeons came to roost in a forest on the banks of the Green River. Farmers traveled hundreds of miles to greet the birds. They came with wagons packed with guns and ammunition. Audubon was among them. His description of the ensuing slaughter is chilling. During the course of one long night, uncountable numbers of the birds were shot with guns or simply beaten from the trees with poles, each man taking as many birds as he had the means to carry. Hogs were let loose to feed upon the considerable remainder. The carnage vastly exceeded any need for food. The hunters would seem to have been driven by pure blood lust. Later, Audubon participated in a buffalo hunt on the Great Plains, a prodigious and terrible taking of life. After shooting his first bull, he cut off the tail and stuck it gaily in his hat. Other hunters smashed open the skulls of animals and ate the brains, warm and raw. On this occasion, the great painter of birds apparently experienced a twinge of remorse: "What a terrible destruction of life, as if it were nothing, or next to it, as the tongues only were brought in, and the flesh of these fine animals was left to beasts and birds of prey, or to rot on the spots where they fell."

He feared lest the buffalo should go the way of the great
auk, a North American flightless bird that had existed in
great numbers, but by Audubon's time had been hunted to
extinction by human wantonness. Until the sixteenth century, great auks populated the islands of the North Atlantic
by the millions. For millennia they had been hunted by the
native peoples of North America, with little effect on their
numbers. Only when Europeans arrived was the bird's fate
sealed. The journals of early explorers often describe the ef-
fortless annihilation of great auk colonies. One seafarer
noted the astonishing ease with which the birds were
driven to slaughter, "as if God had made the innocency of
so poor a creature to become such an admirable instrument
for the sustenation of man." And not just for "sustenation,"
but also for malicious, useless murder. Audubon possessed
only one authentic record of a great auk caught on American shores during his lifetime, a bird snared on a fishing line
by the brother of his engraver. His painting of great auks
depicts a creature so apparently benevolent and gentle it is
hard to comprehend the magnitude of the unfeeling avarice
that brought about the bird's extinction. Curiously, the
final depredations of the great auk were commissioned by
"naturalists." The few remaining refuges of the birds were
sought out by paid agents of individuals and institutions in-
tent upon expanding their collections of avian skins and
eggs—all, of course, in the name of science. The last-known
surviving pair of birds was taken in June 1844, on Eldey
Rock off the coast of Iceland, by agents of a collector. In the
course of capture the pair's solitary egg was smashed. Thus
did the great auk pass into oblivion.

Among Audubon's watercolors at the National Gallery are many of sweet tranquillity and gentleness. I was especially drawn to the sad, wise face of the great gray owl and the great egret with a tail like a flow of water. But I came back again and again to the red-tailed hawks engaged in bloody battle for the hare, perhaps because they reminded me of the taking of the pigeon I had witnessed a few days earlier. Violence is a necessary, generative part of nature, neither moral nor immoral. It is only to human acts of violence that we apply ethical judgments. Most of us do not fault Audubon's use of a gun on behalf of his art and science, but we shrink from the unrestrained slaughter of pigeons, buffalos, and great auks. In this regard, not even Audubon escapes our censure. The passenger pigeon followed the great auk into extinction. The buffalo survives, but barely. Since Audubon's time, many dozens of species of birds, amphibians, reptiles, mammals, and fish have become extinct in the United States. The unnecessary slaughter of the innocents continues. It is a kind of violence that in all of nature is uniquely human.

 New Moon

One of my students came in from the field with a blueberry gall. "What is it?" she asked. I explained that it was an abnormal growth of the blueberry stem caused by a tiny wasp with the mellifluous name *Hemadas nubilipennis*. The adult wasp lays its eggs on new growth in early summer. The larvae hatch, burrow into the stem, and secrete a chemical that causes the blueberry plant to grow a lumpish swelling, which usually distorts the twig into a U shape. In the cozy interior of the gall, a dozen or so wasp grubs pass the winter. In spring, they nibble their way to just under the gall's skin, metamorphose into adult wasps, and push out into the world. If you find a gall later in the season, I said, it will be riddled with escape tunnels, each a millimeter or so in diameter. The gall found by my student was from last season, with a full complement of holes.

I retained the gall and placed it on a corner of my desk. After a while, it began to take on a familiar aspect—a little man, with escape holes for eyes, a crease for a mouth, and protruding bits of blueberry stem for limbs. Then it dawned on me who the man was: Joseph Merrick. I fetched a biography of Merrick from my college library, with pictures of the subject drawn from life. I placed the blueberry gall next to the pictures: the likeness was striking.

Joseph Merrick is known to history as the Elephant Man. He looked—well, like a blueberry gall. Huge lumpish growths on his head, back, buttocks, and legs. Slabs of reptilian skin. Twisted bones. One arm was slender and normal, the other a grotesque tuber. He was healthy in mind, with normal genitals and sexual appetites, but nonetheless so monstrous in appearance that he ignited fear and loathing in all who saw him.

Merrick was born in Leicester, England, in 1861, and was abandoned by his mother to a workhouse at age three or four. As a young man, he allowed himself to be exhibited as a freak as his only way of making a living. In his twenties, he was "rescued" from this odious fate and given a room in which to live at London Hospital. Even the hospital nurses could not bear to look at him. If he appeared in the street without a mask and all-covering cloak, a riot was sure to follow. The Victorians were fascinated with Merrick. In his hospital chamber, which was called the Elephant Room, he was visited by members of the medical establishment, celebrities, and even royalty. They gawked; they were repelled; they spoke platitudes. He caused in them, one imagines, feelings of smug superiority, an opportunity to practice their Christian charity, to love (or pretend to love) the utterly unlovable. Fascination with Merrick has continued into our own century. He was the subject of several books — one by the doctor who rescued him from public exhibition, another by the famous anthropologist Ashley Montagu. He inspired an award-winning play by Bernard Pomerance and a film by David Lynch, both called *The Elephant Man*. Merrick endures as a cultural icon because his very existence challenges our faith in the goodness of nature.

We assert piously that "beauty is only skin-deep," but we believe in our heart of hearts that physical brokenness sometimes denotes a moral flaw — if not of the broken person, then of nature itself. The word *monstrous* means both "deformed" and "evil." We ask: What lapse in creation allows cells to run so hideously amok as to turn the body of a man into something so bizarre? What evil twist of genes gives rise to a man with the soul of an Ariel and the body of a Caliban? We can't seem to accept this terrible brokenness in a human life without evoking the action of a malignant Satan, or a God who sees and punishes our secret sins.

The gall manikin on my desk suggests another interpretation. The disfigurement of the blueberry plant has no moral subtext. A wasp deposits an egg. A larva excavates and secretes. A genetic chemistry is disturbed. The resulting deformity has been perfected by nature over millions of years. The blueberry plant is not significantly disadvantaged by the gall; the wasp achieves an edge in the struggle to survive and reproduce. For all its strange appearance, the gall is no more good or evil than the peacock's feather or the orchid's blossom, or any other product of evolution. Only in humans do we count the disfigurements of genes or disease as morally debased. The agents of disfigurement — viruses, bacteria, or aberrant genes — are following scripts written into their chemistry. Merrick's body was awry at birth. A genetic flaw made his thin frame the bearer of ghastly gall-like growths. No God punished him. No Satan intervened. The script for that poor man's misfortune was in the DNA of his wretchedly fissioning cells. The chemistry of life is not animated by love or justice or pity. Humans can love nature, but we are not loved by nature in return. Joseph Merrick died in his sleep at age twenty-nine, suffocated by the burgeoning excrescence of his own head.

 First Quarter Moon

On nature walks with students, I have often used my penknife to open galls on blueberries, goldenrod, oaks, cherries, and willows, to expose the larvae of wasps, gnats, and midges. At the center of each gall is one or more tiny larvae. If I did not interfere, the following spring each larva would have metamorphosed into an adult and escaped its place of winter repose into the world. Usually, having opened a gall, I nudge the larva from its nest with the tip of my knife. Together, we examine it with a magnifier as it turns and twists in the palm of a hand, and marvel that this speck of maggoty flesh might have become, in the fullness of the next season, a delicate flyer with wings. Then, lesson finished, I drop the larva to the ground.

I have noticed recently that I am slightly discomfited about opening galls. A twinge of regret bubbles up from somewhere deep inside. I am not a sentimental person. I swat flies and trap mice. I eat the flesh of mammals, birds, and fish. And I know, as I nudge a larva from a gall, that insect life is based on an excess of fecundity; a vast and indiscriminate mortality is part of the plan.

And yet, and yet . . .

Let me see if I can tease a worthwhile moral from this potentially mawkish beginning.

No scientific issue evokes more passionate controversy than animal rights. Huge numbers of animals are used and destroyed in biomedical research and education. American researchers alone use something like forty thousand monkeys each year, more than one million dogs, cats, rabbits, and guinea pigs, and fifteen million rats and mice. Scientists vehemently defend the use of these animals as an absolute prerequisite to progress in human healing. Animal rights activists just as vehemently deplore the "misuse" of animals in research. Most of the research is unnecessary, they say, and much of the rest could be done with tissue cultures or computer simulations.

The climactic episode in the animal rights controversy came in 1984 when members of the Animal Liberation Front, a radical organization, broke into the laboratory of Thomas Gennarelli at the University of Pennsylvania and stole videotapes of head injury experiments on baboons. Gennarelli was studying the kind of brain traumas that occur in certain automobile accidents, when the brain is slammed against the inside of the skull. His goal was the better treatment of such injuries and the saving of human lives. In Gennarelli's experiments, the animals' heads were placed in plastic helmets, then struck with a mechanical piston. Not a pretty thing to watch. People for the Ethical Treatment of Animals, another animal rights organization, edited more than seventy hours of stolen tapes down to a horrifying twenty minutes. The widely disseminated edited video was a huge propaganda coup for the animal rights movement and stoked passions on both sides of the issue. That the tapes were obtained by burglary caused many scientific researchers to become even more determined to counter what they consider to be emotional and ill-considered appeals to the court of public opinion.

It would take a book to set out the ethical pros and cons of animal experimentation (two good ones are Deborah Blum's *The Monkey Wars* and F. Barbara Orlans's *In the Name of Science*). The animal rights controversy is not one of good versus evil. Rather, two virtues—knowledge and love—are here in apparent conflict. Society will be best served if both sides in the controversy concede some

measure of virtue to their opponents. Animal rights activists must recognize that knowledge gained from animal
experimentation might lessen the total amount of suffering
in the world, by leading to better healing arts and an envi-
ronmentally educated public. And scientists must concede
that knowledge is not an absolute virtue. As the turn-of-
the-century naturalist John Burroughs said, "To know is
not all, it is only half. To love is the other half." It has always
been my hope, as I opened galls with my students, that this
tiny sacrifice on behalf of knowledge would lead them to a
greater love of nature. I once suggested something like this
in one of my *Boston Globe* columns. A young reader wrote in
response: "If you're not ready to switch places with the one
you're hurting, then it's not right. It's that simple. When
you sacrifice another's well-being, even for a good cause, it
doesn't just mess up the one you hurt. You also screw up
your own soul (or heart, or mind, whatever), regardless of
the positive results your action may seem to have. When
you had that feeling of regret as the larva fell to die, it
wasn't stupid. It was compassion. There is no wisdom without it." The letter touched me deeply. I do not believe the
matter is as simple as the reader suggests, but I know that
when compassion is in immediate conflict with knowledge,
we had best lean toward compassion. That, as she says, is
wisdom.

My walks to and from work each day take me through
land administered by the local Natural Resources Trust. It
was there, a few weeks ago, that I met the deer. A rainy
November evening. Early twilight. Three young deer—
yearlings—lamp-eyed and cotton-tailed, were feeding in

the rain-wet meadow. They ran from my approach. The next evening they watched warily from fifty yards away. The third evening they approached near enough to hear my whispered admiration. The fourth evening, responding to my entreaties, they came to within a few yards. If I had had a carrot in my hand, I believe they might have taken it from me. Then it dawned on me. I was not doing these animals a favor. In satisfying my desire to feed on their beauty, I was increasing their vulnerability. A tame deer is an easy shot. So I began avoiding them. I went out of my way *not* to be friendly. Once, I even hooted to frighten them away. Then, the next evening, they were gone. Later, I discovered their fate. A hunter entered town land adjacent to the Natural Resources Trust reservation. He set up a stool and sat down to wait. When the three yearlings came near, he shot two. A dog took the third. What am I to make of this? I have friends who are hunters and also passionate amateur naturalists who hunt legally and responsibly. I could not hunt myself, and cannot imagine how anyone with an ounce of compassion in his heart could shoot a yearling deer from a stool. But I have no qualms about eating meat, and I have gone on record defending animal experimentation in science. There is a broad spectrum of opinion regarding the taking of animal life, from the lab-bombing terrorism of radical antivivisectionists, to the blast-anything-that-moves attitude of some irresponsible hunters. We must each find our own place on the spectrum.

Never has the question of animal rights been more controversial than today. The antivivisectionist lobby is powerful and well financed. In the United States and in Europe it has forced adoption of guidelines and laws regulating the use of lab animals. Under pressure from the animal rights lobby, schools and colleges are rethinking the dissection component of introductory biology courses, finding ways to exempt students with moral qualms about dissection. In some cases, computer simulations are substituted for actual dissections. Scientists generally welcome regulation of animal experimentation. The number of animals used in research decreases each year. Furthermore, sympathy generated for animals by animal rights activists may serve science on another front.

The preservation of biodiversity, the variety of life on Earth, has become a high priority for all scientists. The planet is undergoing an extinction event comparable to the catastrophe sixty-five million years ago (apparently caused by the impact of an asteroid) that eliminated the dinosaurs and countless other species of plants and animals. The present catastrophe is of our own making, and only respect for life on a broad scale can prevent sweeping extinctions. In *The Diversity of Life,* Harvard biologist E. O. Wilson quotes the Senegalese conservationist Baba Dioum: "In the end, we will conserve only what we love, we will love only what we understand, we will understand only what we are taught." The task of science today is to learn as much as possible as quickly as possible about those species that are threatened, and to share that knowledge with as broad an audience as possible. That's what I am attempting to do when I open galls with my students. Whether love follows knowledge remains to be seen.

These thoughts about the rights of animals are evoked

by that tiny larva squirming in the palm of my hand. I sacrifice its life in the cause of knowledge and of love, that my students may be better citizens of the more-than-human world. But increasingly, as I get older, the balance of love and knowledge tips more insistently toward love. Call it sentimentality, call it wisdom—who knows? I remember what Thoreau said of fishing: "I have found repeatedly, of late years, that I cannot fish without falling a little in self-respect. . . . I have a skill at it, and, like many of my fellows, a certain instinct for it. . . . But always when I have done I feel that it would have been better if I had not fished. I think that I do not mistake. It is a faint intimation, yet so are the first streaks of morning."

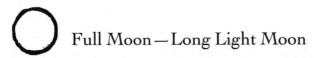 Full Moon—Long Light Moon

Let me pose one of the most important philosophical questions of our times: what is a weed? OK, I'm being facetious, but not entirely so. Before we get to the philosophy, let's go for a walk outside.

Lately, I've been trying out a new field guide, Carol Levine's *A Guide to Wildflowers in Winter*. Never mind that the winter's first snows have bludgeoned the fragile stalks of many erect plants into the ground. There is still plenty that is interesting to see among the dead or dormant plants of winter, and Levine is a useful guide. I also have Lauren Brown's older, more familiar *Winter Weeds*, a book that I have used with pleasure for many seasons. Brown's book is not as comprehensive as Levine's, and the key is somewhat harder to use, but her plant descriptions and her drawings have an engaging charm. Every "weed" listed in Brown's book is also included among Levine's "wildflowers." Which raises the perennial question: what is a wildflower, and what is a weed?

My dictionary defines *weed* as a plant considered unattractive or troublesome, especially one growing where it is not wanted. Clearly, since the two authors describe the same plants, the dictionary definition was not enough to help them decide on the title of their respective books. Are weeds unattractive? It is the *attractiveness* of many winter weeds that makes them such pleasures to observe; in winter, the exquisite machinery of plant reproduction is often highlighted in crisp brown relief for our appreciation. Troublesome? Scarlet pimpernels are no trouble— indeed, they are welcome wherever we find them—yet they are listed in my little Golden Guide *Weeds*, wherein weeds are defined as "successful plants that nobody wants." Lady's slippers are among the most eagerly anticipated plants of the spring, yet here they are among Lauren Brown's "weeds." Phragmites, those tall plumelike reeds we see in marshes at the side of the road, are pernicious and usurping invaders, yet they are included among Levine's "wildflowers."

Many handbooks define a weed as "a plant out of place." This assumes that we know the proper place for a plant. Dandelions are considered out of place in a lawn, but from a Darwinian point of view a dandelion in the lawn is very much *in place*, a flawless adaptation of plant to habitat.

The Golden Guide to weeds emphasizes their adaptability to diverse and adverse circumstances, such as the dandelion's ability to survive even in cracks in concrete. One secret of a weed's success, says the guide, is its efficient means of reproduction, including prodigious numbers of seeds equipped for dispersal with parachutes, hooks, or spring-loaded catapults. This "efficiency" is often trouble for us, like those annoying seeds of the beggar-ticks we must pick off our clothes. Other books emphasize the small, unshowy blossoms of weeds, as if they were the ugly ducklings of plants.

The concept "weed" can be usefully extended beyond the plants. Most of us would categorize starlings as animal weeds. Some of us would apply the term to the white-tailed deer that invade our backyards. Are houseflies, brown rats, and bedbugs weeds? Try this definition: a weed is any species of life adapted for prolific colonization of disturbed habitats, often displacing indigenous species.

Now you can probably guess where I'm heading. Let's ask what species is best adapted for intruding its burgeoning progeny into every nook and corner of the planet, displacing other species of plants and animals, driving many to extinction. You've got it: the human weed. We are the weed par excellence. We disturb habitats, then move in, with our camp followers, the lesser weeds. We are the dandelions in the lawn of life, forcing indigenous species from the field. Conservationists bemoan declining populations of elephants in parts of Africa and blame poachers and the ivory trade, but it's not just lust for ivory that threatens the elephants, it's proliferation of the human weed into habitats that previously belonged to the elephant. Nothing is happening to African elephants that has not already happened to indigenous North American and European species. Americans and Europeans tend to be self-righteous about conservation in other parts of the world, but only after we have already decimated our own wildlife. We are the weed that did in the great auk, the passenger pigeon, and nearly the bison, too.

The concept "weed" carries enormous emotional and ethical baggage, especially when expanded to include animals as well as plants. Philosophers of nature would do well to study the etymology of the word, and its moral implications. Until we have figured out what is a weed and what is a wildflower we won't understand our proper place in nature. And unless humans can somehow escape our biological imperative and get our burgeoning population under control, the day will come when we will live on a planet inhabited by nothing but weeds.

 Last Quarter Moon

"In wildness is the preservation of the world," said Thoreau, and his felicitous phrase has become something of a mantra for conservationists. But what did Thoreau mean to preserve? What do *we* mean to conserve?

Thoreau said, "Give me a wildness whose glance no civilization can endure": another mantra, much quoted by conservationists. What does it mean? Thoreau used the phrase in his journal as a snappy put-down of his oh-so-civilized neighbors. Then, in his essay "Walking," he used the phase again: "Give me a wildness whose glance no civilization can endure,—as if we lived on the marrow of koodoos devoured raw." What an image! The philosopher of Concord hunkered down on the African veld, hair unkempt, half-naked, extracting antelope bone marrow with a stick, his chin running with blood. More likely to find him dabbing his lips with linen in Emerson's dining room. "Hope and the future for me are not in lawns and cultivated fields, not in towns and cities, but in the impervious and quaking swamps," he wrote, and we know we are listening to far-fetched rhetoric, a crazy, cockeyed dream. He wouldn't have survived a week alone, without the accoutrements of civilization, in, say, the Okefenokee or the Everglades. He returned from the relatively tame Maine woods happy to be back in the thoroughly tame landscape of Concord.

This conflicted nonsense from Thoreau rubs off on many present-day conservationists. Against civilization they posit the tonic of wildness—nature unsmudged by the rapacious hand of humankind, a primeval pre-Eden paradise where the rivers run free and the lion lies down with the lamb. But, of course, in the real wild world, the lion has the lamb for dinner, and the rivers are bloody arenas of eat or be eaten. Every species, with one exception, has a single objective: get mine. Selfishness is built into creation from the genes up. If the wilderness presents an appearance of harmony, it is because millions of years of deadly competition have produced a balance of power—a standoff of mutually assured destruction. The poet-conservationist

Gary Snyder writes: "Wilderness is a place where the wild potential is fully expressed, a diversity of living and nonliving beings flourishing according to their own sorts of order." That's the Thoreauvian romantic speaking. In fact, "their own sorts of order" can be reduced to one invariable law: nature red in tooth and claw.

The romantic view of wild nature is extended by many conservationist writers to hunter-gatherer human societies, and particularly, in this country, to extolling Native American wisdom as the antidote to our environmental problems. We should not forget, however, that the first hunter-gatherer peoples to arrive on this continent, at the end of the last Ice Age, were apparently implicated in the greatest mass extinction of large animals the continent has ever seen—at least since the age of the dinosaurs. Native American experience and wisdom should be valued, as we value all historical traditions, but they will not save wildness, any more than they keep snowmobiles and all-terrain vehicles out of Native American garages or frozen TV dinners out of Native American refrigerators. Show me a person of any cultural background who prefers raw kudu marrow to a Big Mac and I'll concede that we have something to learn from hunter-gatherers about saving the environment. The first fact we have to accept is that science and technology are not going away. Human technological domination of this planet is the bottom line where every conservation ethic must begin. The untrod wilderness is finished, kaput. Whatever happens in the forest, mountains, desert, or sea will happen by human design. Even Thoreau knew this: in a journal entry for August 30, 1856, he wrote, "It is vain to dream of a wildness distant from ourselves."

So what do we want to save? No species other than our own could even ask the question. Only humans have evolved the intelligence to imagine an escape from nature's dogma of immediate self-interest. Call it civilization, call it wisdom, call it a recognition of a power and mystery that transcends the agenda of any individual species, call it whatever you want, but it means we are effectively free to create the kind of environment we want. And what we apparently want is more and more technology, but with protected enclaves of natural beauty—forest parks, wild rivers, nature preserves. We want a house in the ever-expanding suburbs, but we also want our children to see a wild condor soaring above a pristine landscape. We want the ersatz glitz of Orlando and the wild egrets of the Everglades.

Balancing these two hankerings of the human spirit will take all the wisdom we can muster and a hearty helping of restraint. Can we have our technology and a taste of wildness, too? Yes, but only if we build an environmental ethic on the evolving wisdom of technological civilization. It is not the experience of hunter-gatherer societies that will save the condor and the egret, but the methods of science. The decisions to be made are social and political, pitching civilized generosity against wild self-interest, scientific ecology against consumerist greed. "We have built a greenhouse, a human creation, where once there bloomed a sweet and wild garden," writes conservationist Bill

McKibben. But the "sweet and wild garden" never existed, and a "greenhouse" may not be a bad thing if it is built with scientific knowledge, compassion, self-restraint, and an eye for beauty. Wildness is not the preservation of the world; it is our own wild nature that is the threat to biodiversity and nonhuman environments.

The solution is to draw upon our more generous impulses, and our hard-won scientific knowledge, to study, love, and protect what in our wild abandon we could wipe out in the blink of an eye.

Each morning I walk to work through land cared for by our town's Natural Resources Trust. It is a tamed landscape, as thoroughly humanized as the fields and woodlots of Thoreau's backyard—an artificial landscape, to be sure, but one created with an eye for beauty, balance, and civility, and it has nourished my spirit for thirty-five years. There is a stream, a water meadow, a swamp, a bluebird meadow, woodlots, rugged outcrops of bedrock. One recent October morning I walked there through meadow mists tinged gold by the rising sun. I crossed the plank bridge over Queset Brook, skirted the water meadow, then took the higher path through the old orchard. And there on the path I met a crayfish, on hard, stony ground, eight hundred feet from the creek and three hundred feet from the nearest mud or water. Crayfish take their name from the word *crevice* and have nothing to do with fish at all. They are freshwater cousins of lobsters and crabs, evolutionary migrants from the salty sea, who like to hide in crevices and burrows. More to the point, they are 100 percent aquatic and mostly nocturnal. So what was this fellow doing out in the open, on dry land, in daylight?

The crayfish was an adult, about six inches long, with lobster claws and a mess of legs. Two BB eyes looked up from the tips of stalks. Somewhere inside that brown exoskeleton was a BB brain not much bigger than the eyes. Not impossible, I supposed, that he was dropped on the path by a heron or raccoon that had taken him from the stream. But his carapace was unbroken, his limbs and antennae intact; no evidence of damage by beak or jaw. He was not in the most robust shape, but by all appearances he seemed to have found his own way into his present predicament. I hunkered down on the path and watched him, prodded him, offered a twig to his lethargic pinchers. This guy belongs in the stream, I thought. I picked him up and walked back to the bridge. I was about to drop him in but then thought, Who am I to say why this fellow was on the path? Crayfish breed in this late season; maybe he is on some amorous mission I know nothing about. So I took him back to his place on the path. But I paused again. No, I thought, some predator must have dropped him here. Back to the bridge, and this time I plopped him in.

For the rest of my walk I wondered: What was that all about? Why so much shilly-shallying about intervention? I wouldn't have given the crayfish a second thought if I met him in a Cajun stir-fry, and I had let myself get sucked into a silly dilemma: to put him in the stream or let him be? But perhaps the dilemma was not so silly after all. My minor moral muddle reflected in miniature a major environmental debate whose outcome will effect the shape of the world to be inherited by our great-grandchildren in the next century: To manage nature, or keep hands off? To address problems of conservation through scientific knowledge and technical intervention, or by the attempted restoration of a presumed natural balance? Greenhouse or "Sweet and Wild Garden"?

Among many conservationists the management of nature is tainted with arrogance and avarice. Wild nature is imbued with a kind of natural morality, they say, a give-and-take harmony. Back in Neolithic times, humans lived as part of a balance that included and respected all creatures. But science and technology have shredded that mystic fabric, driven God from the wild temple. "If we can only step aside and trust in nature, life will find a way," says a character in Steven Spielberg's movie *The Lost World: Jurassic Park.* He speaks for those who would keep hands off.

On the other side of the debate are the managers— nature's keepers—who believe the only way to save natural environments is to apply principles of scientific ecology. Even those environments we think of as wild and free are products of tens of thousands of years of human intervention, say the keepers. Untrod nature is a romantic myth, and letting nature have its way won't save a single threatened species or natural environment. What is required is management based on sound ecological research. "No matter what we choose to do, nature is shaped by man," says environmentalist writer Stephen Budiansky. "We can accept the fact and try to deal with it, or we can ignore it and accept the consequences. The one thing we cannot do is remove human influence simply by closing our eyes to it."

Do we put out forest fires caused by lightning, or let them burn? Do we cull deer herds, or let them multiply unchecked? Do we build jetties to save eroding beaches, or let the sea have its way? These are difficult questions, and so far the record of success by the nature managers has not been impressive. On the other hand, incessant hectoring by prophets of environmental doom has done nothing to reverse the course of technological civilization and turn us back to Neolithic ways, nor will it.

My own feeling is that management is the only way forward and that we had better learn a lot more good ecological science, fast. Human domination of this planet is a fact of life that is not going away, and the idea of nature as separate and wild is bankrupt romanticism. If we want our great-grandchildren to have access to natural environments and maximum biodiversity, we should put our taxes where our mouths are and support the acquisition and application of scientific ecology. What we need are more and bigger nature preserves, protected rivers, national parks — artificial to be sure, as artificial as the Bronx Zoo or Central Park, but better than a world paved over with tract houses, malls, and asphalt. As ecologist David Foster makes clear in *Thoreau's Country: Journey through a Transformed Landscape*, Thoreau not only recognized the extent to which his landscape was humanized, he actually reveled in the civilized character of the land. "The wilderness is simple, almost to barrenness," he wrote in his journal; "the partially cultivated country it is which chiefly has inspired, and will continue to inspire, the strains of poets."

The planet Earth will become increasingly humanized; nothing will reverse that trend. Extolling wildness as the preservation of the world will get us nowhere; what is required is the political and social will to create landscapes that are works of art, spirit, praise.

And the crayfish? God knows what was his fate. But I'm glad I intervened. All things considered, my little act of ecosystem management was probably good for crayfish — and maybe good for my great-grandchildren, too. If nothing else, those brief moments during which I entangled my life with another creature drew me deeper into a recognition of what we stand to lose. Neither letting the crayfish be nor dumping it into the stream contributed mightily to resolving our conflicted hankerings for both technology and wildness, but such prayerful acts, multiplied ten million times over, might just provide a societal basis of knowledge, love, and restraint that will allow us to shape on this planet an artificial garden that will nourish the human spirit and continue to inspire the strains of poets.

In civilization is the preservation of the world.